# CELTIC GREATS

Paul McStay and Roy Aitken brandish the 1988 Scottish Cup that completed
Celtic's Centenary year 'double'.

# CELTIC GREATS

### HUGH KEEVINS

*Foreword by*
JOHN C. McGINN

JOHN DONALD PUBLISHERS LTD
EDINBURGH

# CELTIC GREATS

*Dedication*

For my mother, Mrs Alice Keevins,
who still worries about them.

ISBN 0 85976 238 6

Phototypeset by Swains (Edinburgh) Limited
Printed in Great Britain by Bell & Bain Ltd., Glasgow

# *Foreword*

My first recollection of watching Celtic in action dates back to the early forties when football was not unnaturally in a state of flux because of the war. I know from older members of my family that I was first 'lifted over' the turnstiles as a small child in the late thirties but I cannot in truth remember any details of games or players. What I can remember is travelling by the number 9 tramcar from Scotstoun to Celtic Park, a journey of 50 minutes via Dumbarton Road, Argyle Street and London Road with the ultimate destination of the tram being Carmyle or Auchenshuggle.

It was, for example, following one such journey that I saw Bobby Evans making his debut in the green and white hoops having joined the club from St. Anthony's junior team in Govan. In his debut Bobby covered every blade of grass playing in the inside left position without making any great contribution to the game for the boundless energy expended. However, on eventually finding his true position in the right half role he went on to become one of the most gifted and famous Celtic half backs of all times.

I also had the privilege of seeing the games in which Charlie Tully and Jock Stein made their debuts for Celtic. From the beginning Tully showed the impish devilment that was the trademark of his career and Stein displayed the leadership qualities that were to be seen throughout his life in football. Alas, both these great Celtic men have gone to their rest.

The other eight great players who are under the spotlight I have known very well as players during my own period with the club. To tell the story of these individual contributors to Celtic would take much more space than was available to the author. Nevertheless, I am sure that all football fans will be as delighted and pleasantly entertained as I was reading this excellent book which highlights parts of their careers.

*John C. McGinn*

# Acknowledgements

My special thanks to the various players who gave up their time to reflect on great careers and to all the others who helped with this book, in particular Pat Woods for his unfailing courtesy and practical assistance, without which the job would have been a lot harder. To Kevin McCarra for his support and to Allan McGraw, Tommy Gallacher, Doug Baillie, John Kelman, and to Hamish Walker of the Scottish Football Association for his help in compiling the players' international careers, my deep gratitude.

The co-operation of Celtic's chairman, Jack McGinn, was much appreciated and I am indebted to him for supplying the Foreword during his relentlessly busy Celtic centenary year.

Pictorially, D.C. Thomson were of invaluable assistance and I am grateful to them.

# Contents

The 'Lisbon Lions' show off the European Cup at Parkhead in 1967.
Back row: Auld, Gemmell, Wallace, Chalmers, Simpson, Craig, McNeill,
Clark and Murdoch. Front: Johnstone and Lennox.

# Introduction

There are as many players worthy of adopting the mantle of a 'Celtic great' as there are supporters of the club willing to articulate their case for inclusion. The European Cup-winning team of 1967 would, for instance, create a strong enough emotional pull on their own for there to be a move to include them *en bloc* and simply thank the rest for all their efforts over the years. Those of a more parochial nature, who believe that the highest form of achievement for any Celtic side is a win over Rangers, whether it is in a fully competitive match or the fourth replay of a West of Scotland Reserve League Cup tie, might opt for those who distinguished the jerseys ten years before Lisbon by running up the record score for a national Cup final in Scotland and beating Rangers 7-1 at Hampden.

In 1988, Celtic celebrated one hundred years of providing accomplished teams to fuel such arguments. In all that time it has never been enough for their supporters that Celtic should merely win at any level, rather it is compulsory that victory is achieved with the flourish that comes from a commitment to attacking play and a willingness to entertain at all times. The burden of upholding this philosophy while paying attention to the practicalities, like remembering that the supporters will still reserve the right to make their displeasure known if worthwhile results are not forthcoming, is an awesome one. Those whose careers in Celtic's post-war era are highlighted within these pages have discharged this dual responsibility in a way that has made their names synonymous with the club's best traditions and granted them reverential status in the eyes of those whose pulse rate quickens whenever Celtic cross the halfway line.

The fact that defenders like Billy McNeill and Danny McGrain are called to the podium for recognition here does not in any way contradict what has gone before, either.

The present Celtic manager, for example, scored goals that helped win three Scottish Cup finals, a distinction which any forward might be happy to take into retirement with him, while McGrain's world renown was based on winning the ball from the other team and then visiting them in their own half of the park as often as the human system would allow lung-bursting runs of eighty yards or so in length. The selfless careers of those two players was, to paraphrase John F. Kennedy's expression to sum up emotional ties, a case of ask not what Celtic can do for you, but what you can do for Celtic.

An element of less well disciplined, even raffish behaviour has never gone amiss at Celtic Park, either, and those who have imposed their personalities on the team in that way tend to be immortalised as well for the uplifting richness of their contribution. For those of us who were brought up in the Glasgow tenements of the fifties, a genuine misapprehension was forgiveable over Charlie Tully. His picture hung on the walls of so many homes and his Christian name was used conversationally with such frequency, that large numbers of young children were in danger of growing up believing Tully to be a blood relation rather than the object of widespread affection. If the legendary Charles Patrick's background as an Irishman who had settled in Glasgow struck a chord with those whose forebears had developed a keenness for Celtic and their unashamed association with the country 'across the water', the club has always been able to broaden its horizons as well and gratefully accommodate those who did not come to them as Celtic men but fostered a lasting feeling for the place.

Jock Stein, who would become Celtic's first Protestant manager in 1965, arrived there initially as emergency playing cover in 1951 and with the vague remit that he might be able to bring on some of the club's younger players. Instead, he was an inspirational force in restoring Celtic's pride with a League Championship win and the taking of the Scottish Cup which, along with the Coronation Cup in 1953, provided the first signs of post-war dignity.

In any analysis of Celtic's one-hundred-year history, Stein would have to be seen as the most important figure of all in the club's development, able to look at a total of twenty-five major competitions won in his thirteen years as manager that elevated an ordinary team to the stage of universal acclaim and was lacking only the official confirmation of their pre-eminence that would possibly have been Celtic's but for the fiasco of the brutal World Club Championship final against Argentinian side, Racing Club, in 1967. What will be a permanent tribute to Jock Stein are the statistics of a World record-equalling nine League Championships in succession and Celtic's place as the first British club to win the European Cup, all of which were achieved by a team that attained respect on an unprecedented level from their adoring followers.

There may even yet be some reserved registrars who have not quite recovered from the shock of being asked to fill out a birth certificate for a child whose Christian and surnames were separated by Simpson, Craig, Gemmell, Murdoch, McNeill, Clark, Johnstone, Wallace, Chalmers, Lennox and Auld. This practice, too, was not always restricted to male children born in the year those men beat Inter Milan and gained immortality.

To lionise — and there seems no more appropriate word — only three players from that side may seem like a desecration of their collective memory but there would surely be nobody who would question that Jimmy Johnstone was a uniquely gifted performer, capable of raising the game to a spectacular level in the face of intimidatory acts against the person of someone who had the build that once earned him the soubriquet of the 'flying flea'.

No such liberties could have been taken, or that descriptive name have been given to Bobby Murdoch. An unfortunate metabolism that would cause him to put on weight at a dramatic rate unless he followed the dietary routine of a jockey eventually brought about Murdoch's downfall at Celtic Park, but not before he had been both the creative and destructive force in what was known then as the right-half position after turning down a weekly wage of £8 from Motherwell as a schoolboy.

This immunity to material forces, the concept of playing for the jersey in other words, is an outmoded idea in an era of freedom of contract and personal agents. It is absolutely true to say, though, that Billy McNeill adhered to the old-fashioned philosophy of one club loyalty, and to the extent, some might say, of acting above and beyond the call of duty. For eight years, during which Celtic won nothing of note and their supporters became known instead as sympathisers, McNeill resisted clandestine approaches to make a name for himself elsewhere. His stoicism was fully rewarded over the next decade of his playing life in the shape of twenty-three different kinds of winners medals. As full of incident as McNeill's playing career had been, however, nothing could have prepared the onlooker for the melodrama that would follow him as manager of the club.

McNeill, though, had been the man who said that Celtic were an exceptional club who demanded extraordinary talents, and in Danny McGrain and Kenny Dalglish they found a pair who would at least have got to sit the entrance exam for the Lisbon Lions of whom McNeill had been a member.

It is one of the commendable features of Celtic that they do not discriminate against players on the basis of anything other than ability. In the earliest years of the club's history there were suggestions that a sectarian policy, excluding all but those of a Catholic persuasion, be adopted, but this was rightly deemed to be unworthy of consideration. McGrain and Dalglish became two Rangers supporters who learned at the feet of the Lisbon Lions and earned the respect of the crowd at Celtic Park for the wholehearted and cerebral nature of their efforts in the cause of a club they were quickly able to espouse.

The captaincy of Celtic passed from those two men in turn into the hands of Roy Aitken in 1986, and if that honour incorporates extra responsibilities at this nostalgic juncture in the club's affairs there will be no reservations over Aitken having the presence to handle all that comes his way.

A tireless competitor, Aitken came to Celtic as a schoolboy from Ayrshire and was so much a part of the first team while still studying for his exams that he required the equivalent of a note from his teacher to get time off to play in a European tie in East Germany in 1976. Given normal luck with injuries, that early start to his career could ensure that Roy Aitken enters the club's record books on some not too distant date as the man who has played more times than any other for Celtic.

All of those whose abbreviated biographies appear in this book spent long years at Celtic Park. There are others who have done likewise and whose omission here in any elongated form is regretted by an author who will now do his best to give an honourable mention to as many as possible of those who are asked to appreciate that, as someone has to be first and last, there sometimes has to be a cut-off point as well.

In deference to their contribution towards Celtic's illustrious history, the rest of the Lisbon Lions take precedence.

Ronnie Simpson came to Celtic nearer, the supporters thought, to pensionable rather than playing age. He became living proof that goalkeepers glow in the twilight of their professional years. For a man who was known to keep himself to himself, Simpson's back-heeled clearance against Inter Milan, performed when he was several yards outside his own penalty area, was among the most flamboyant gestures in that match and summed up the side's immunity from stultifying nerves.

Jim Craig was a subtle defender and is a walking authority on the club who has a special line in anecdotes on those times when Celtic could do hardly any wrong. On one of the rare occasions they did, Craig, coincidentally, was missing. Motionless in what he thought was the role of an innocent bystander as Jock Stein berated the playing occupants of the dressing room, the manager suddenly turned on him and uttered the memorable words, 'And as for you, Craig, you must be some player if you can't get a game in this team!'

Tommy Gemmell was one of the most colourful characters to wear a hooped jersey. Famed for his adventurous play and the ferocity of his shooting, 'big Tam' made the game look what it is supposed to be, a source of entertainment.

John Clark probably never made a fuss about anything in his life, and that included being the innocent victim of the upheaval that led to managerial changes at Celtic Park in 1983. 'Luggy', as he was known, tiptoed around the park being a big noise in the best side of the lot without anyone hearing about it.

Willie Wallace was sold to Celtic by Hearts in what was surely an oversight on the part of the Edinburgh club. In the first six months of his career with Celtic, 'Wispy' scored 25 goals in 29 games, including the two that won the Scottish Cup final against Aberdeen and the pair that carried the club into the European Cup final. In four complete seasons, he never failed to score less than that quarter of a century each time, making him an inspired buy.

Steve Chalmers still works for Celtic as part of their development company and will be remembered for all time as the man who scored the winning goal in Lisbon. Even Billy McNeill, when asked in the course of the research into this book, could not hazard a guess at what age Steve was when he gained that distinction, and detective work is not helped by the fact that, however old he was in 1967, Steve still looks the same age today.

Bobby Lennox was the last of the European cup-winning team to leave Celtic as a player. He was still winning cup medals there in 1980, ten years after he had won European football's prized bronze boot award for scoring 32 league goals in a single season. Now the reserve team coach at Celtic Park, where he is known to all as 'Lemon' for the outsize grin that is permanently set on his features, Bobby Lennox made his birthplace of Saltcoats famous for something other than buckets and spades.

And then there was Bertie Auld, or 'Ten-thirty'. The original gallus Glaswegian, Bertie was Charlie Tully incarnate in the way he infuriated defenders with cunning artistry. A caricaturist's dream with his jutting jaw, Bertie provided the author with an early insight into playing to the gallery when he shook hands with a fan who had wandered on to the pitch before taking a corner kick at Celtic Park.

There has rarely been an individual as committed to the ideal of Celtic being as much a way of life as a football club as Tommy Burns. During the League Championship of season 1987-88 that saw the club celebrate its one hundredth year in such an extravagant style, there were days when the burden of what they were trying to do became almost too heavy for the team. One such occasion was a home game against Morton in February, when it required a last-minute penalty from Roy Aitken to avoid the loss of an unexpected point. When I asked Tommy Burns afterwards how he had viewed the day's events, he said it was a case of 'kisses from Heaven'. The supporters know what he is talking about and they reserve a special place for him in their affections as the player who was born and brought up in what was the cradle of the club in the East End of Glasgow and deeply respects their origins and motivations while being one of the finest talents to wear their colours as well.

Death, especially one that is tragic and premature, can lead to the creation of a legend, but the late Johnny Doyle had already carved out a niche for himself with the Celtic supporters before being killed in a household accident in 1981. Celtic like to think of themselves as the people's club and Johnny Doyle thought only of himself as the 'supporter with a strip'. Johnny had a brightness of wit and personality that was stronger than the Celtic Park floodlights. Once he suggested to the manager, Billy McNeill, that, as he had been honoured by being made a Member of the British Empire, Doyle himself should be recognised, not for services to football but for being good company. There would have been no argument if someone in authority had invented such an award.

If it is an advantage for any individual to have a strong sense of the club's identity, it is also an undeniable truth that it is easier for a player to make his name against Celtic than it is to establish a reputation with them.

Johnny Doyle came to the club from Ayr United, and while he may not have been technically the most advanced of players, he did make the transition assuredly. Davie Provan and Murdo MacLeod were two others who came from clubs in a lower division, Kilmarnock and Dumbarton respectively, and took a significant part in revitalising Celtic under Billy McNeill in his first stay as manager. Provan's career was, of course, cut sadly short because of debilitating illness, but it was an indication of the high esteem in which he was held that a crowd of well over forty thousand turned up on a bitterly cold night in

December, 1987 to bid him farewell and to watch the symbolic moment early in the game with Nottingham Forest when the retiring player handed over his jersey with an embrace to his substitute, Joe Miller.

MacLeod had left Celtic months before to join the German club, Borussia Dortmund, and it was again in keeping with the recognition of services rendered that even though he ultimately played his part in eliminating Celtic from the U.E.F.A. Cup there was a queue of players, directors and supporters to be seen forming in the stand of the Westfalenstadion to wish Murdo good fortune before they set off for home.

There have been others who left Celtic under less satisfactory circumstances, but it should not be forgotten that players like Charlie Nicholas, Brian McClair and Maurice Johnston were identikit pictures of the archetypal Celt for the discerning supporter, being lithe and invigorating forwards whose only interest was in creating discomfort in the opposition penalty area. McClair was Celtic's top goalscorer in each of the four seasons he spent at Celtic Park, while Nicholas made such a profound impression on the fans in a short space of time that it has to be recalled that he played in only 111 competitive matches, during which he scored the remarkable total of 64 goals. You could take the boy, like Nicholas, out of Glasgow, but you could not take Glasgow Celtic out of the boy, and Charlie was at Nottingham five months after his move to Arsenal with a green and white scarf peeking out of his pocket on his way to support the team against Brian Clough's side in the U.E.F.A. Cup.

David Hay was manager of Celtic by then, and if there are valid doubts that can be expressed over the suitability of his temperament for that job, what is not a matter for debate is that as a player in the late sixties and early seventies David Hay wore Celtic's jersey with great distinction. The same compliment could be paid to Jim Brogan, who worked on the theory that if Celtic did not have the ball the team would not get very far and went out to take it from the opposition with a fair-minded determination that implied 'Brogie' would have run through re-inforced concrete if necessary.

Both Brogan and Hay were fortunate in playing for Celtic during the Stein era, which was the equivalent at times of having direct access to the magic wand, but there were others whose careers came in between that post-war period and the big man's arrival as manager who occasionally made it look as if the team were not struggling at all, which was a not inconsiderable trick during the lean years.

Willie Fernie had a belief in attacking play that was turned into an ideological approach to club management with Kilmarnock, even if he took it all the way to the loss of his job for refusing to put safety first. Decades before the club thought of putting Celtic's story on stage in the form of a musical, Fernie was setting the game to music with his mellifluous style of play and keen eye for goal. Neil Mochan, now part of Celtic's backroom staff, had a ferocious shot and the type of disposition that caused him to be known as 'smiler'. Bobby Collins was small but as strong and as intelligent a player as the club have had.

John Hughes may not have been the purist's idea of how the game should look but he was compulsive viewing when he worked up a head of steam and also had a deftness of touch that belied a frame big enough to see him go throughout his time with Celtic known only as 'Yogi Bear'. These were all household names in sides who had only sporadic success, but had it on their own, and the club's, terms.

There were also the tragic cases. Joe McBride was Jock Stein's first signing as Celtic manager and promised at one time to be the most memorable as well. In his first season and a half, Joe played 78 games and scored a stunning 77 goals. A knee injury then diminished his effectiveness and saw to it that McBride took part in only twelve games over the next season and a half before he was eventually sold to Hibs.

Physical problems are one thing, but to lose a commodity as valuable as George Connolly because of external considerations that have nothing at all to do with the game itself is much harder to take. Connolly was capable of doing anything with the ball, except, perhaps, eat it, and even that was never proved conclusively. He was, though, from a small village in Fife and could not kick the country dust from under his shoes.

At the end of the 1972-73 season, George was named Scotland's Player of the Year. Eighteen months later, hopelessly miscast as a prominent personality in a city as devoted to its football as Glasgow, George, who had once confided in a teammate that his real ambition had been to become a long-distance lorry driver, announced his decision to give up the game.

One hundred years of a club like Celtic could not have been negotiated without running the full gamut of emotions from high achievement to low farce, bitter tragedy to sweet memories. The organisation that was formed essentially to feed the needy has inspired its followers to ingest the names and the outstanding stories of the past, and a rich history it is, too. Billy McNeill, the only fitting occupant of the manager's chair in their centenary year, believes Celtic to be the underdogs in their own city in spite of passing innumerable milestones like the Exhibition Cup, the St. Mungo Cup, the Coronation Cup, the European Cup and the one hundredth Scottish Cup as well as the feat of winning nine League Championships in a row. This would dovetail with the supporters' perception of themselves and the team they follow. It is the stuff of romantic notion and the imperishable belief that talent will out. An extraordinary club in every sense of the word.

## CHAPTER ONE

# *Charlie Tully*

It is not by ability alone that a Celtic player becomes revered in the eyes of the support, or has his memory cherished long after his days with the club are at an end. Talent is the basis on which adoration is earned, but to be possessed of other attributes that impinge the individual on the consciousness of the faithful is to be admitted to the select few who have had legendary status bestowed upon them at Celtic Park. The post-war prototype of the species was Charles Patrick Tully.

Some people are born great, some acquire greatness and others have greatness thrust upon them. The genial Charlie would probably have said that he was a favourable combina-

Charlie Tully: First of the post-war legends.

tion of all three! He arrived in Glasgow from his native Belfast at a time of post-war austerity and introduced impudence when that commodity was as much in a state of short supply as anything else to those holding on to their ration books.

The Celtic following in particular were hungry for a hero in whom they could invest their sorely tried affection, and Tully gave them everything they wanted to see or hear. If the latter meant playing games with the truth as much as the former involved doing the same with opposing professionals, then Charles Patrick Tully was, as they said in the country of his birth, your man.

Even his biographical details contained the occasional feint to avoid the truth in order to provide a better story. The fact of the matter was that Charlie was the second of twelve children born in McDonnell Street, off the Falls Road, to Charles and Mary Tully in the late afternoon of July 11, 1924. Later, in a series of first person articles written for the Dundee *Courier,* he would claim to have come into the world to the accompaniment of 'drums booming and flutes tootling' on the twelfth of July and allege that this was how his birth was celebrated on the streets of Belfast. This was a case of journalistic licence taking precedence over the transcripted evidence of his birth certificate, since the marching bands were out in force commemorating an anniversary of a more established vintage!

Devilment was his game, though, and Tully was at the head of the band who led Celtic out of their depression after the Second World War and won the club, in 1951, their first Scottish Cup in fourteen years and then took them on to their most successful season in four decades three years later.

If Mary Tully was the matriarchal head of a family that consisted of seven boys and five girls, it was only her maternal instincts that brought about, indirectly, this particular son's arrival in Glasgow, seemingly destined to play for Celtic. The young Tully, a precocious talent on the football field, had made his debut for the now defunct Belfast Celtic at the age of fourteen years and nine months against a Glentoran Select. His natural ability was such that Arsenal had expressed a wish to bring him to London on a trial basis but his mother, showing a healthy regard for her offspring's welfare, had deduced that even the irrepressible Charlie might not be able to do anything about avoiding the Luftwaffe's assault on that city and counselled against such a move.

Being a member of a large family breeds independence in other ways, though, as Tully had shown in developing his skills as a football player in the first place. His school, St. Kevin's, had allowed only the national game of hurling, a robust pursuit only marginally less dangerous than the attentions of the Luftwaffe, but Charlie's preoccupation with football had caused him to scour the public parks of Belfast in search of a game where there might be a team who were a man short.

By this circuitous route, he was introduced to the headmaster of another school who found him an outlet for his obsession by getting the teenager a place as a ball-boy at Belfast Celtic's Grosvenor Park. While playing for Forth River in an amateur league, Tully was spotted by Elisha Scott, a legendary former Liverpool and Northern Ireland goalkeeper, who was then manager of Belfast Celtic, and invited to join the club on a more orthodox basis than catching the ball for others.

By 1947, and having recovered from a gland operation which prevented him from travelling with the Irish League team to play their Scottish counterparts at Celtic Park, Tully had scored the goal that won the Irish Cup final for Belfast Celtic over Glentoran. Taking part in a five-a-side tournament run by the Royal Ulster Constabulary, Belfast Celtic then lost only narrowly to a visiting Rangers side including 'Tiger' Shaw, Torry Gillick and Willie Thornton.

Satisfied that rumours of the player's ill-health were completely without foundation, Celtic revived their interest in signing Tully to the extent that, a few days later, the club's omnipotent chairman, Bob Kelly, and his manager, Jimmy McGrory, went over to Belfast and returned with his signature on a transfer contract for a fee of £8,000 and with the promise of a house for Charlie and his fiancée, Carrie, in Glasgow after their wedding. Two weeks later, Charlie Tully arrived quietly at the Broomielaw in Glasgow for pre-season training. If the entrance down the steps of the *Royal Ulsterman* was unspectacular, the effect of his coming on Celtic, and the team's supporters, would be profound.

In the season that had gone before, Celtic had lived with the ignominious prospect of being relegated from the First Division for the first time in the club's by then sixty-year-old history. Only a mediocre total of nine matches had been won out of a possible twenty-nine when the side travelled to Dens Park to fulfil their last fixture, against Dundee. Popular mythology has this as the game which formally saved Celtic from demotion. In fact, a defeat might not have been the same as pulling the switch on the trapdoor leading down to the lower orders but would have involved a fraught wait for those beneath them, Queen of the South, Morton, Airdrie and Queens Park, to complete their programme before finding out who went down.

Nevertheless, the hat-trick scored that day by Jock Weir, the last goal of which was scored two minutes from the end and won Celtic both points, was received like a reprieve from the warden as the Glasgow contingent in a crowd of 31,000 behaved in a demonstrative way uncharacteristic of the people in sensible overcoats and caps who then populated the terracings.

Tommy Gallacher, son of the legendary Patsy, another who, like Charlie, needed no other form of identification beyond his Christian name in conversation among Celtic supporters, had played for Dundee that day. Now retired after many years involved in writing about football as a journalist, Tommy can recall the impact Tully was to have straight away on a club recovering from that narrow escape.

'Charlie came to Scotland at a time when wingers were speed merchants, with players like Willie Waddell of Rangers and Hibs' Gordon Smith. What he lacked in pace and strength, Charlie made up for in other ways, like taking the ball right up to the full back and showing that he was a masterful dribbler. He would also signal with his hands where he was going to put the ball next in order to exasperate his opponent. The supporters had never seen anything like him and he became their idol, saviour even. No player gets that much praise for so long unless he is doing something to deserve it, though, and Charlie

The supporters had never seen anything like Tully.

Tully was one of the Scottish game's greatest characters.'

Tommy Gallacher's testimony is generously given, considering that he can also recall Tully being responsible for his getting booked for the first time in his professional career.

'By his own admission, Charlie never used to get a kick of the ball when he played against me, and during one game I dispossessed him, ran forward and made my pass. As I did so, Charlie ran by and blatantly tripped me up for my cheek. By the time the referee turned round to see what the fuss was all about all he caught was my retaliation!'

It would take him until the end of his third season for Tully to use his wiles more productively on Celtic's behalf. He scored the goal that defeated Raith Rovers in the semi final of the Scottish Cup and eye-witness accounts say that this act, nine minutes from the end of the game, was his only conventional kick at the ball all day as he gesticulated, flicked and domineered his way throughout a match that brought Celtic back to Hampden where a John McPhail goal gave the club that trophy for the first time since 1937.

Tully's investiture as the prince of players at Celtic Park was held at the national stadium later that same season when, in the final of the St. Mungo Cup devised to celebrate the Festival of Britain, a piece of impertinence from him helped win the game. Two goals down to Aberdeen and going into the final minute of the first half, Celtic were awarded a throw-in near the bye-line. In the absence of more orthodox assistance, Tully elected to throw the ball off the back of the unsuspecting Aberdeen defender Davie Shaw, thereby gaining a corner kick. Shaw remonstrated with the referee, Jack Mowat, but his protests went unheeded and from the corner, which Tully took himself, Sean Fallon scored at a crucial moment. After Fallon had scored again to equalise early in the second half, a cross from Tully, elated that his earlier mischief had worked, to Walsh won the cup for Celtic.

Some thought Tully's unprecedented tactic unsportsmanlike. The Celtic suport, emotional at being re-united with success on the playing field, took no part in the public debate and developed Tully-itis instead. Extreme sufferers asked for, and got, Tully cocktails in the pubs and special, green-coloured ice cream in the cafes to take away the taste of the bad years. If the term had been in currency at the time, Tully would have been known as a cult figure, and jokes about him began to proliferate.

When Celtic went on tour of Italy, it was said that the pilgrims filling St. Peter's Square in Rome looked up at the balcony of the Vatican and asked who it was standing beside Tully. At home, the story went that Tully did not need to pay income tax because he had ten dependents, meaning the other mem-

Tully displays the style that caused an outbreak of Tully-itis!

bers of the Celtic team. If all of this was meant to convey the impression that the great man had been delivered of paranormal powers, he chose the very earthy surroundings of Falkirk's Brockville Park to give his disciples additional fuel for their arguments.

At a point in the Scottish Cup tie there when Celtic were two goals behind, a seemingly hopeless position from which Tully tended to take sustenance rather than discouragement, he took a corner kick that went straight into the Falkirk goal. The referee, Doug Gerrard, either suspecting that such a practice ran contrary to the laws of nature or that Tully was bending the rules of the game by improperly positioning the ball outside the arc before taking his kick, ordered a re-take in front of a restive crowd who had spilled on to the track around the playing surface.

Feigning surprise at the decision and perplexity at how he was to handle the constricted space, Tully handed the ball to the linesman to place it for him on the arc. When he then performed what seemed like the miraculous by scoring direct once again, the spectators invaded the field, giving full vent to their feelings of ecstasy, and after order was restored Celtic went on to win the game by the odd goal in five. Falkirk's vice chairman, Willie Turner, dismissed the phenomenon by saying it could not happen again 'for another twenty years'. In actual fact Tully had already performed the identical trick some months before while playing for his country against England. Having deceived the highly respected goalkeeper, Gil Merrick, another disbelieving referee defied Tully to do the same thing twice, only to find out dares were like the stuff of life to a player at the peak of his creative powers. His strategy at corners was simple: if the award was to be taken from the left-hand side of the field, Tully took it with his right foot and vice versa. That he had a strategy at all would have surprised those who thought of Tully as an entertainer first of all and then as a tactician only in that he knew in which boot to place which foot. The man himself was, admittedly, scornful of those who overdid the theorising, believing that 'everyone has only one pair of legs and one pair of arms'. As age slowed him down, though, astute distribution of the ball became his strength, as he demonstrated in the Coronation Cup tournament of 1953.

It was said that Celtic, who were on the rebound from a disastrous season domestically, were only being invited to face such as the then English champions, Arsenal, because of their exceptional drawing power in Glasgow. A crowd of 59,000 assembled at Hampden for their first game to prove the point, but the huge assembly also witnessed the triumph of determination over reason as a Bobby Collins goal with a Charlie Tully patent marked on it, being direct from a corner kick, put Celtic into the semi finals against Manchester United. The gate swelled to 73,000 and saw Tully engineer the first of Celtic's goals for his fellow Ulsterman Bertie Peacock. For the second, Tully controlled a long clearance from the full back, Rollo, and in one movement had the presence of mind to flick the ball over the head of a United defender for the ever-alert Neil Mochan to score. Hibs were met, and beaten, in the final and from little expectation there grew out of that competition the basis of a side who would then provide three years' worth of sustained achievement.

The League and Cup double of the following season represented the club's best performance in forty years and the winning of the League Cup by Celtic for the first time since its
inception came after that, once Tully had finished choreo-
graphing the emphatic defeat of Partick Thistle which arrived
with three goals in a six-minute spell.

There are some Celtic supporters, however, for whom the
relevance of counting up what had gone before, or what could
be hoped for in the future, lost all meaning on October 19,
1957 when they experienced the pinnacle of life's achievement
and Charlie Tully basked, for the final time, in the warmth of
their appreciation at the highest level.

Celtic's 7-1 win over Rangers in the League Cup still stands
as a record score for a national final and will forever be recalled
by the less cosmopolitan, non-European minded of their supporters as the club's finest hour. It was also Tully's farewell to
the winners' rostrum at Hampden. He had taken the quickest
route to the hearts of the Celtic following by destroying
Rangers in his first Old Firm match nine years earlier, but it
would not have been Tully had he not had a story to tell sur-
rounding his swansong as well.

In his newspaper column in the now discontinued *Evening
Citizen,* Tully had said the Scotland international side, in which
Bobby Evans was centre half, contained only two players entitled to be thought of as world class, neither of whom was the
redoubtable Celtic captain. The offending piece of part-time
journalism was pinned to the wall of the home dressing room
with appropriately barbed comments written underneath for
Tully's benefit. For once his good humour deserted him and
Irish blood overheated to the astonishment of fellow players as
a full-scale fist fight then ensued between the two men only
forty-eight hours before the final with Rangers. The last word
on the subject, though, was not written or spoken, rather it was
mimed by Tully as he gestured where he was going to put the
ball to a demoralised Ibrox defence who knew what he was
doing but were powerless to intervene. To this day the final
score is still daubed for posterity on buildings and bridges in

the West of Scotland, but for Tully writing of another sort was on the wall.

Portly, balding and at the veteran stage in any case, Charles Patrick Tully played his last competitive match for Celtic on October 1, 1958, almost a year after putting the final touch on an imperishable memory. Twelve months after that he was appointed player-manager of Cork Hibs in the Republic of Ireland. He took them to the final of the Football Association of Ireland Cup in his first season but ended up part of the losing side against Shelbourne at Dalymount Park in Dublin.

His last appearance as a player in Scotland came when, at the age of thirty-six, he was chosen to play for the League of Ireland against the Scottish League at Celtic Park, which may have accounted for the healthier than usual crowd of 23,500 who seemed to congregate for old time's sake and to take a lingering look at what was once a treasured acquisition.

Management jobs with Bangor and Portadown in Northern Ireland came next before Charlie died on July 27, 1971. He had been working as a sales representative for a whisky firm and had gone back to Bangor to take over part-time control of the side. He passed away in his sleep aged only forty-seven years old.

Thousands of people lined the Falls Road in Belfast as the funeral cortège made its way to Milltown cemetery, where the coffin was partly borne by Jock Stein and Billy McNeill, then Celtic's manager and captain respectively.

Charlie Tully was more than just a crowd pleaser but it was his spirit that endeared him to a people who used a bit of cheek as a safety mechanism as well as a source of light relief. The generosity of his spirit is summed up in one last story about him, for once not apocryphal and certainly not of his own creation, it having often been said of Tully that if there were no good tales about him going around Glasgow, he would make one up himself for circulation.

Six months after his death, and appearing unobtrusively as lot 229 in the catalogue inside the auction rooms of J. Davidson and Company of Bath Street in Glasgow, Charlie Tully's Scottish Cup runners up medal from season 1954-55 was up

The inimitable Charles Patrick; A 'Great Celt.'

for sale. He had given it to a friend as a memento. The late Celtic chairman, Desmond White, paid £19 for something that had a face value of £5. It was bought for the club's trophy room because the medal had a 'great deal of sentimental value for us. Charlie Tully was a great Celt.'

## FULL INTERNATIONAL CAPS

| | | | |
|---|---|---|---|
| **1948** | | | |
| Oct. | England | (h) | 2·6 |
| **1949** | | | |
| Nov. | England | (a) | 2·9 |
| **1951** | | | |
| Oct. | Scotland | (h) | 0·3 |
| **1952** | | | |
| Oct. | England | (h) | 2·2 |
| Nov. | Scotland | (a) | 1·1 |
| Nov. | France | (a) | 1·3 |
| **1953** | | | |
| Apr. | Wales | (h) | 2·3 |
| Oct. | Scotland | (h) | 1·3 |
| **1955** | | | |
| Nov. | England | (a) | 0·3 |
| **1959** | | | |
| Oct. | Spain | (a) | 2·6 |

Northern Ireland score first.

CHAPTER TWO

# *Bobby Evans*

There is a long-established saying which has it that a player only gets out of the game what he puts into it. The lengthy and inspiring career of Bobby Evans would call that particular piece of homespun philosophy into question, all the way to suggesting it has no basis in fact at all. In going from teenhood to middle age as a professional, Bobby Evans never earned any more than twenty pounds a week. If that meant he was never allowed to make a fortune out of assembling forty-eight caps at full international level for Scotland, twenty-four appearances for the Scottish League as well as two Scottish Cup, one League Championship and two League Cup winners medals,

Bobby Evans: Fit, skilled and sporting, the definition of the traditional Celtic player.

the affable Evans was at least rich in praise for being the definition of the traditional Celtic player, in that he was superbly fit,
highly skilled and habitually sporting.

If Charlie Tully was the embodiment of the club's cavalier
spirit, Evans typified the intelligence that made him an equally
essential part of the post-war side, and one who was able to
sustain his tireless and aggressive style throughout the whole
of the fifties as well. In a Celtic team that was hardly a model of
consistency during that period, Evans was a constant source
of strength whose forte lay in anticipating the actions of the
other side and then starting a counter attack with a passing
ability that was sorely underrated.

What is indisputably true is that Celtic have never spent the
meagre sum of five pounds so wisely on any individual. That
was all the club paid to Evans' father in 1944 when the then
seventeen-year-old made the transition from amateur to professional status in a matter of weeks. Originally a Third Lanark
supporter from the South side of Glasgow, Bobby had started
out playing for Thornliebank Methodists. During one especially competitive match, totally lacking in the spirit of fellow-
ship, Bobby caught the eye of Tommy Pilton.

He was a Dumbarton player of the time who was out of the
side because of injury and had therefore turned into an itiner-
ant spectator in search of a game near his home in Barrhead.
Pilton's sphere of influence extended to the committee of St.
Anthony's, a junior club in Govan, and it was on his recommen-
dation that the small, red-headed forward was signed. After
less than a dozen games at that level, Evans' potential was so
obviously noticeable that Jimmy McStay, then Celtic manager,
made him his last signing before leaving the club.

'But for Tommy Pilton I might never have got the opportunity to play the game for a living and would probably have finished serving my apprenticeship as a joiner,' he says today,
using that fortunate sequence of events to explain why he
enjoyed his football so much and rarely, if ever, took umbrage
at opponents. 'It was all an accident and I remained grateful
that one lucky break should have enabled me to have such a
long and fulfilling professional life.'

Tireless, aggressive and a constant source of strength.

Any gratitude Bobby experienced in return certainly did not come from the Celtic support in those early days, however. Evans was more used to his performances being decried from the terracing as Jimmy McGrory, his second manager, moved the small bundle of energy from one position to another, trying to find out where he would be most comfortable. In all Bobby took up nine different places in the team, including twice standing in as goalkeeper as a result of injury. If he were not naturally gifted in all of them, Evans' athleticism inevitably saw him through in the end. As a young man he was known to play three rounds of golf in the same day as well as being a strong swimmer who was equally at home with a badminton racket in his hand as he was with a ball at his feet.

All of these pursuits were designed to strengthen the parts of his body that football would not and, as a consequence, his energy could have been genuinely described as boundless. If his ambition had no limitations, either, Bobby's arrival at Celtic Park coincided with a period that was fallow enough to starve even the most optimistic. Evans was resilient to a fanatical degree, however, and the fact that out of this mediocrity in his everyday place of work he became the most regularly capped player at the club spoke volumes for his level of determination.

Before he had experienced the sensation of winning a trophy with Celtic, Evans made his Hampden debut in 1948 for Scotland against Northern Ireland, who then came complete with their legendary forward, the so-called Red Fox, Peter Doherty. As Scotland went two goals down in the opening minutes of the game the crowd, and some of the more experienced players in the home side, became discernibly cowed by the course of events but the young Evans almost single-handedly rallied those around him. Doherty was subdued by ferocious tackling, and meticulous passes started to find their way out to the right-wing partnership of Rangers' Willie Waddell and Jimmy Mason of Third Lanark. Eventually Scotland made a complete recovery and won the game by the odd goal in five, with Evans being the deciding factor and totally unconcerned that he ought to have been too immature for that kind of salvage operation.

Before the term became fashionable, Evans was the perfect example of the power of positive thinking, and prior to the dawn of the fifties he had already won over the Celtic crowd who had once reviled his name. By then, in fact, they expected him to be the mainstay of the team, regardless of how the results were running, and for the most part they were running in the opposite direction from Celtic.

'I always believed that the only difference between a bad team and a good one was two fine results,' he says, expounding a theory that has not altered since Evans found out at first hand what it was like to change from one to the other. The transformation was brought about after he had once again proved to be the indomitable character of the team as Celtic won the Coronation Cup in 1953. Beside him by then was Jock Stein at centre half and soon they would be joined by the Ulsterman, Bertie Peacock, to form one of Celtic's greatest ever half-back lines. Stein was the composed defender, unhurried on the ground and assured in the air, while Peacock possessed a subtle creativity that was perfectly complemented by the hard-running industry of Evans on the opposite side from him.

The three games it took to win the Coronation Cup proved the veracity of Evans' words about how quickly a team's personality could be changed. In the season that followed Celtic won both the Scottish Cup and the League Championship and Evans missed only one match in the process, for all that his father felt his son was being harshly treated by opponents.

'He never played football himself but he was always encouraging me to give back as good as I was getting in the physical sense. The way I answered him was to get up and walk around the centre of which ever room in the house we were sitting in, proving to him that no lasting damage had been done. I would say to him, 'I can still walk, can't I?', and that would be the end of the discussion.'

For a fully paid-up professional, albeit a poorly paid one in the days of the maximum wage, there was more than a touch of the old Corinthian spirit about Evans. In fifteen years with Celtic, Bobby was never sent off and was booked only three times.

On two of these occasions Jack Mowat, a strict referee of military bearing and one who would not have won any personality contests among the Celtic support in any case, was the official in charge. One of Mowat's cautions was actually administered after the ninety minutes' play was over, when Evans' sense of injustice was sufficiently outraged to have him call a decision into doubt after time had run out. The biggest miscarriage of justice, however, took place at Love Street against St. Mirren in an ordinary league match there.

'I had been fouled three times by the same player while running with the ball, all of which went unpunished. When I eventually managed to make my pass, I turned away from everyone and took a harmless swipe at fresh air in my frustration. Then, to my astonishment, the referee called me over and brought out his book. His name was Peter Fitzpatrick and he was a Celtic supporter into the bargain, in fact that was the sole reason for me being cautioned. He told me that with a name like his he had to book me or the crowd would think he was biased in our favour.'

It was during a Scottish Cup tie at the same ground, though, that there arose one of the most famous incidents associated with Bobby Evans and his time in the game. He had halted a promising attack by St. Mirren when his hand prevented a pass reaching one of their forwards, Gerry Baker. A few days later, Bobby's action was denounced in a letter to the correspondence columns of the now defunct *Evening Citizen* as being 'unsporting'. The very idea was more than Evans' flesh and blood could stand and, armed with a copy of the newspaper bearing the correspondent's name and address, he set out with his wife for Paisley in order to defend his good name in person.

'It took three separate visits before darkness fell until someone eventually answered the door and I could finally point out to my critic, man to man, that he could say anything at all about my capabilities as a player but I strongly objected to being called unsportsmanlike. I also asked him if he would have preferred me to let the ball run to my opponent and then watch me kick the feet from under him. There was no answer to that and

Time was always on Bobby Evans' side over twenty years at the top.

on the way home I wondered if someone had put the poor man up to drafting the letter, maybe even someone who worked for that newspaper and wanted to have a go at me in an indirect manner.'

Slow to anger on the field, Evans worked on a short fuse off the park when he smelt injustice where he was personally concerned. It was always his opinion that a rash of criticism about his form for Celtic would break out, anything but coincidentally, just as the Scotland selectors were about to pick the national side.

'I still believe to this day that if I had played for any other club but Celtic I would have won far more international caps than I did, perhaps as many as twenty more. There were times when players I knew were inferior to me were picked and often from the most obscure places while I was under the noses of the Selection Committee and recognised as playing well up until a couple of weeks before they met.'

This feeling of persecution became so acute that Evans eventually exploded and wrote to the Scottish Football Association telling them that he would prefer not to be chosen for his country. Bob Kelly, who was then Celtic chairman, had questioned the wisdom of that step but Evans was not the type given to second thoughts.

'The only aspect of the whole business which upset me were the headlines in the newspapers that said, 'Evans does not want to play for Scotland.' I had stated in my letter that while the selectors had angered me I would, if selected after that, naturally turn up and give of my best, as always.'

Evans did so, after a short absence, in 1955 when he took over at centre half for his club as well as his country, replacing George Young of Rangers for Scotland and Jock Stein at Celtic Park when an ankle injury that was to finish the career of his team-mate prematurely first became apparent. Undoubtedly smaller than is usually considered healthy for that position, Evans brought his positional sense, concentration and predatory instincts to bear and was never exposed as having any shortcomings. He retained his place all the way to the 1958 World Cup finals in Sweden with Scotland, who went out from a section that also involved Yugoslavia, Paraguay and France.

His time at the top did not have long to go, however, and in 1960 Bobby Evans left Celtic Park after an internal dispute which he still finds difficult to get over even now. He chose not to discuss the intimate details of that row within these pages because two of the central characters involved in the whole story, both members of the Celtic board of directors at that time, are now deceased, and as he says with that keenly developed sense of fair play, 'Dead men can't answer back for themselves'. What is patently obvious is that, whatever the nature of his disagreement with Celtic, the memory still angers him today and had nothing at all to do with the club wanting the young Billy McNeill to take over at centre half, one of the popular misconceptions of the time. Bobby Evans signed for Chelsea and tried to settle in London but he was very quickly on his travels again and became manager of Newport County.

In March, 1962, he was allowed to go from that job by

'mutual consent' and returned to Scotland to play again, this time for Morton, with whom he also took up a position as coach to the younger players. It was at this point that Bobby came into contact with Allan McGraw, one of the Greenock club's revered names for his goalscoring exploits. In six seasons at Cappielow, McGraw scored over two hundred goals for Morton and he would give much of the credit for that distinction to Bobby Evans.

'I was newly returned from doing my national service and it was about the time when training for professional teams was beginning to take on a more serious, carefully thought out, aspect, rather than just endlessly lapping the track. Bobby hated shirkers and those who went through the motions were not forgiven. Even when he was well into his thirties, Bobby still had an awesome will to win and it was not uncommon for the normal day's training to finish with a five-a-side game that could last as much as two and a half hours, longer than training itself, until Bobby's team had won. Where he helped me in particular, though, was in improving my ability in the air. Many people failed to notice that Bobby's balance and timing were such that he hung in the air waiting for the ball long before such as Denis Law became renowned for doing the same thing. He also taught me that a goalscorer, and he had tamed a few in his day, lives by his instincts, going where he believes the ball will eventually come to him. By listening to both pieces of advice, I was top scorer at Cappielow in every one of the seasons I was there and took most of them with my head.'

'So far as I am concerned, Bobby never got the credit he was due and was forgotten about by Scottish football. The game let him down because he had an awful lot to pass on and he never got the chance. I always said that if I got into management I would have him with me in some capacity and in 1985 I asked him to join Morton as a scout but he couldn't take up the job for family reasons.'

After Morton, and before that offer to go back to Greenock, there then came the most traumatic phase in Bobby Evans' life. He joined Third Lanark as player-coach but lasted only eleven months before being let go for 'economic reasons' in

1964. In the eccentric ways of that club when it was well into its death throes, Bobby returned to Cathkin just one month later, this time as player-manager. He was the eighteenth occupant of the manager's office in forty-four years, a disastrous average that claimed yet another victim one year later when it was decided the club could not afford a full-time person in charge of the team. Evans resigned and, remarkably, returned to the full-time playing side of the game with Raith Rovers, offering further testimony to his extraordinary standard of fitness at the age of thirty-seven.

Under the management of George Farm, Evans, as captain of the side, eventually led Raith to promotion to the old-style First Division in season 1966-67. Farm had seen Evans' experience as vital to the learning process of his young players at Stark's Park. The departure of Farm and the introduction of Tommy Walker as manager signalled the end of Bobby Evans' twenty-four season long career, however. The two men, who, strangely enough, both enjoyed the reputation of being gentlemanly, never saw eye to eye and within months, in December, 1967, Bobby announced his retirement at the age of forty. Though he had lost his place in the side, Bobby felt fit enough to continue playing, but being forthright to the very end he would not stay where he was not wanted and moved out of football into the world of insurance.

Reflecting on a professional career which had spanned twenty-three years, Bobby said at the time, 'I have been lucky, I don't smoke and I don't drink and I have never had a serious injury. The worst thing that happened to me was getting a slipped disc.'

The words turned out to be a cruel temptation to fate. In July 1969, while working as an insurance collector in Easterhouse, Bobby collapsed suffering from a stomach haemorrhage and was so seriously ill that at one stage his family were told there was nothing more that could be done for him after six days in intensive care. It was precisely because of the exemplary lifestyle he had led up until then, though, that he was ultimately able to pull through and lead a relatively normal, if somewhat restricted, life. It was five years from the time of his collapse

Evans' balance and timing helped him tame a few strikers.

before the doctors would let him work again and his once favourite pastime of golf had to become a thing of the past. Today he works as a storeman in the town of East Kilbride, where he has lived for the last fourteen years.

It was while looking at a game for Allan McGraw when he was considering joining Morton as a scout that Bobby saw his last ninety minutes in person.

'I am not one of those who believes that standards of play began to drop as soon as my era was over, though. The talent is still there in Scotland, as it always was.'

There are no regrets, either, that he was never given the opportunity to work with those promising players in a managerial capacity. Bobby Evans is now healthier and stronger than he has been for some time, besides which he believes recriminations to be a waste of that energy. At Celtic Park he had been signed by one manager, Jimmy McStay, for whom he had a high personal regard but scant experience on a professional level to help make any considered judgement. Evans was allowed to go by another manager, Jimmy McGrory, for whom he had nothing but praise.

'I always felt he was shy, though, and rarely at ease with players. If you were talking about anything other than football, he could be a relaxed conversationalist but the minute the game itself came up he would change the subject. Team talks were always brief and to the point and invariably ended with Mr McGrory going to the dressing room door, opening it and then passing some convivial remark to each player as he made his way out on to the pitch. Our full back, Mike Haughney, was always last out and he told us that the manager's parting words to him would be, 'Well, cheerio then, Mike.'

There was among them at Celtic Park, though, one for whom the subject could not be changed away from anything other than football.

'He would share a room with me wherever Celtic went and it would not be the first time that I have fallen asleep in the early hours of the morning listening to him unload his ideas on how the game should be played.'

He was Jock Stein.

## FULL INTERNATIONAL CAPS

**1948**

| | | | |
|---|---|---|---|
| Oct. | Wales | (a) | 3·1 |
| Nov. | N. Ireland | (h) | 3·2 |

**1949**

| | | | |
|---|---|---|---|
| Apr. | England | (a) | 3·1 |
| Apr. | France | (h) | 2·0 |
| Oct. | N. Ireland | (a) | 8·2 |
| Nov. | Wales | (h) | 2·0 |

**1950**

| | | | |
|---|---|---|---|
| Apr. | Switzerland | (h) | 3·1 |
| May | Portugal | (a) | 2·2 |
| Dec. | Austria | (h) | 0·1 |

**1951**

| | | | |
|---|---|---|---|
| Apr. | England | (a) | 3·2 |
| Oct. | N. Ireland | (a) | 3·0 |

**1953**

| | | | |
|---|---|---|---|
| May | Sweden | (h) | 1·2 |
| Oct. | N. Ireland | (a) | 3·1 |
| Nov. | Wales | (h) | 3·3 |

**1954**

| | | | |
|---|---|---|---|
| Apr. | England | (h) | 2·4 |
| May | Norway | (h) | 1·0 |
| May | Finland | (a) | 2·1 |
| Nov. | N. Ireland | (h) | 2·2 |

**1955**

| | | | |
|---|---|---|---|
| May | Portugal | (h) | 1·0 |
| May | Yugoslavia | (a) | 2·2 |
| May | Austria | (a) | 4·1 |
| May | Hungary | (a) | 1·3 |
| Oct. | N. Ireland | (a) | 1·2 |
| Nov. | Wales | (h) | 2·0 |

**1956**

| | | | |
|---|---|---|---|
| Apr. | England | (h) | 1·1 |
| May | Austria | (h) | 1·1 |

**1957**

| | | | |
|---|---|---|---|
| May | West Germany | (a) | 3·1 |
| May | Spain | (a) | 1·4 |
| Oct. | N. Ireland | (a) | 1·1 |
| Nov. | Switzerland | (h) | 3·2 |
| Nov. | Wales | (h) | 1·1 |

| 1958 | | | |
|---|---|---|---|
| Apr. | England | (h) | 0·4 |
| May | Hungary | (h) | 1·1 |
| June | Poland | (a) | 2·1 |
| June | Yugoslavia | (a) | 1·1 |
| June | Paraguay | (a) | 2·3 |
| June | France | (a) | 1·2 |
| 1959 | | | |
| Apr. | England | (a) | 0·1 |
| May | West Germany | (h) | 3·2 |
| May | Holland | (a) | 2·1 |
| June | Portugal | (a) | 0·1 |
| Oct. | N. Ireland | (a) | 4·0 |
| Nov. | Wales | (h) | 1·1 |
| 1960 | | | |
| May | Poland | (h) | 2·3 |
| May | Austria | (a) | 1·4 |
| June | Hungary | (a) | 3·3 |
| June | Turkey | (a) | 2·4 |

## CHAPTER THREE

# *Jock Stein*

There can be no doubt that Jock Stein was the biggest single influence on Celtic in the club's now one hundred-year-old history. The chairman of the club with whom he would help lift a team from parochial appreciation to international renown, Sir Robert Kelly, was fond of describing big Jock to anyone who would listen as the 'greatest football manager in the world'. When, in 1968, Stein was the honoured guest of the Celtic Supporters Association at their annual rally he was praised on the cover of the brochure for the evening as the 'Manager of the Century' and there would have been nobody there who would

Jock Stein as he was in 1951 when he joined Celtic from Llanelli.

Stein (right) with his wife, Jean, and Charlie Tully after Celtic had won the Scottish Cup in 1951.

have taken that claim to be excessively boastful, merely a statement of fact.

And yet much of what Jock Stein achieved for his beloved Celtic — and the catalogue of accomplishments in thirteen years as manager comprised a staggering ten League Championship titles, eight Scottish Cups, six League Cups and, of course, the European Cup — had its origins in a playing career at Celtic Park that was unremarkable but shaped his approach to the game. It would not have been possible to put together a book dealing with the Celtic Greats and somehow manage to omit Jock Stein, but for all that, apathy greeted his arrival at Celtic Park. His time there is mentioned, at best, as an incidental in any retrospective on his career, as if people found it hard to reconcile the ordinariness of his attainments at that level with the extraordinary milestones that marked his years in the manager's office inside the same surroundings.

In that rhetorical style of speech that was one of his trademarks, Stein would probably have said, 'There's nothing to be gained from looking back, is there?' The inextricable link, however, is that Jock Stein played the game for Celtic as he would eventually teach others to play it on their behalf, using common sense first of all. He also had a detestation of losing that followed him all the days of his life, whether as a player or a manager, and what he was began to take shape only when he signed for Celtic and played for the first time as a full-time professional.

Jock Stein, though, was a late developer. He did not play a trial for his first senior club, Albion Rovers, until he was twenty years of age. It was wartime and the opposition, ironically, was Celtic. The local junior player from Blantyre Victoria who had lived relatively nearby in Burnbank and was a miner, had struggled initially to find the pace of the game as Celtic contrived a three-goal lead. Once Stein had found his bearings, however, he began to exert his personality on those around him and that extensive deficit was brought under control and ultimately converted into a respectable 4-4 draw. Celtic were then so mediocre a team that as much was made of their shortcomings as Albion Rovers' power of recovery, but the manager at Cliftonhill, Webber Lees, knew enough about what had really gone on not to let Stein slip from his grasp and signed him on straight away.

The Southern League that passed for organised competition during the war was a hard school for any young man to come by his education in the game. As a miner, Stein was excused serving in the army but not excluded from the difficult-

As a manager Stein was called the best this century — and nobody connected with Celtic thought that was boastful.

ies of doing the most exacting manual work, and playing football, on what were, quite literally, short rations. The only staple diet Stein knew was regular beatings on the field but the experience was to be character-forming. It bred in him an obsession with giving of his best in the face of adversity and created within him a high level of tolerance for the underdog as well. In eight seasons with the club he made 236 appearances for Albion Rovers and helped them win promotion to the First Division in 1948.

Inevitably, relegation followed, though, and Stein moved on to the Welsh non-League club, Llanelli, being made captain of the team, as he was everywhere he went.

Leaving his wife, Jean, to look after their young daughter,

Ray, in a council house in Hamilton was an unsatisfactory domestic arrangement, though, made even more so by a couple of
break-ins to the family home. Exasperated by the second of
these, Stein was on his way to see the Llanelli officials and tell
them why he had to return home when he found them coming
in the opposite direction with word of an offer from a Scottish
club.

As he said himself on more than one occasion, Jock Stein,
with his particular background, could not claim that Celtic
were his first love, unlike so many of the team's players, but
they were to become the 'last and most abiding'. Some sec-
tions of the support saw his transfer for £1,200 as a big club
buying small, while others, infatuated with the personalities of
the day like Tully, John McPhail and Bobby Collins, found his
signing lacking in inspiration. Celtic had won the Scottish Cup
months before his arrival in November, 1951 and there was so
much resting on laurels that the side was reclining in a dangerous position near the foot of the league table.

If there were reservations about his lack of pace and his
basic ability, there could be nothing said about Jock's qualities
of leadership. Stein's influence always surpassed his talent on
the field of play and, for him, there were only two basic guide-
lines to be followed. The first was that the things a player could
do he should do to the very best of his ability. The second was
that those things which were outwith a person's capabilities
should be left to someone else. These would become the twin
pillars on which Celtic's dominance from the mid-sixties to the
mid-seventies was founded. In 1951, though, there were more
pragmatic targets to be aimed for, like a league position befitt-
ing the club's status and then the pursuit of something more
rewarding.

Luckily, as it turned out for Celtic, both Jimmy Mallan and
Alec Boden were injured in the same week that Jock signed
from Llanelli and so the management were forced to dispense
with the idea that Stein might be gainfully employed at the start
helping to bring on the youngsters in the reserves. It was
necessary for him to make his debut against St. Mirren, and
although he was 'all left side and no greyhound', as one team-

mate had succinctly put it, Celtic Park would never be quite the
same again from that moment on.

Willie Thornton was by then nearing the end of a lengthy
career with Rangers that had ensured him legendary standing
and he could fully understand the value of what Stein was
doing for his greatest rivals.

'I would say that Jock Stein was entitled to be thought of as
being invaluable to Celtic long before he became their
manager. He was precisely the kind of person everyone wants
to have on their side and even then, without saying this in hindsight, I could see he was a natural coach. Jock would be the
chief tactical adviser to Celtic in an Old Firm game as well as
the perfect diplomat. He would delegate people to stop my
runs in on goal while Jock would personally intervene if it
looked as if Celtic's most volatile temperament, Charlie Tully,
was going to fall out with Sammy Cox, who had the shortest
fuse on the Rangers side. In all my time in the game, too, I
never heard one person say that Jock's knowledge of football
and the ability to put it into practice was not all it was cracked
up to be, and that is unusual in this business where there is
always one who thinks he knows better than anyone else.
Equally, I have never heard of the player who failed to pay attention to Jock because they thought a man with only one league
Championship medal and one Scottish Cup winners medal
could not possibly teach them anything. This can be a notor-
ious failing among some of the biggest internationalists in the
game but the likes of Denis Law wept openly at Jock Stein's
funeral and I know that Graeme Souness idolised the big man
as well.'

Stein had begun so effectively at Celtic Park, in fact, that the
then captain of the club, Sean Fallon, had appointed him as his
vice captain, his right to choose being still a tradition within the
club at that time. The charisma of the ex-miner who knew all
about the value of comradeship and the effectiveness of a unit
pulling for each other from his days in the pits where it was 'so
dark all you could see was the inside of your head', was spread-
ing. Fallon had chosen Stein in preference to his fellow Ulsterman, Bertie Peacock, and then, after suffering a broken arm,

Stein (right) with Sean Fallon,
who was at his side as assistant
manager throughout the
greatest days of Celtic's history.

was eventually replaced as captain by his second-in-command.

Stein led Celtic to the Coronation Cup in 1953 and then, in the season that followed, helped them to win the double that was to signify the club's most successful period in decades. There were two incidents in the course of that memorable campaign, during which Celtic lost only one point at home out of fifteen matches played there, that perfectly illustrated Stein's wholehearted approach. On December 12, 1953, while playing against St. Mirren, a penalty kick was awarded against Celtic which gnawed at Stein's sense of fair play. The taker was Davie Lapsley, whose *modus operandi* on these occasions was to begin his marathon run up to the ball from the other side of the halfway line, leaving a team-mate to place the ball on the spot for him as he made the long trek back to his imaginary starting line. Hurtling towards the ball, Lapsley suddenly found himself confronted by the not inconsiderable form of Stein, standing strategically in his line of approach about ten yards outside the penalty area.

The bemused St. Mirren player was forced to make a size-able detour and lost all sense of rhythm, along with his bear-ings, as he emerged from the other side of Stein and hope-lessly misplaced his penalty to the uproarious delight of the crowd. It is worth noting that Celtic were already four goals ahead when this piece of gamesmanship occurred. Stein was completely unrepentant afterwards, observing that 'the rules say I have to give my opponent ten yards at a penalty kick. Where does it say I have to give him fifty?'

The only point mislaid by Stein's team at Celtic Park was conceded against East Fife in a game from which he was able to win a notable legal point from the S.F.A. in return. Celtic had squandered a two-goal lead against the Fifers, the equaliser coming from Charlie 'Legs' Fleming ten minutes from time. As the disgusted Celtic captain retrieved the ball from the net, Stein kicked it forty yards upfield with his right foot. It was pop-ularly accepted, even by his most fervent admirers, that Stein's right leg was only there to prevent his body from taking an invo-luntary collapse to the left-hand side. This was not a view shared by the referee, however, who promptly booked him for the deliberately provocative gesture of striking the match official.

Outraged, Stein appealed against the caution and was brought before the S.F.A. It was there he explained that it was common knowledge his right foot was purely for standing on and could not possibly have been used as the trigger with which to accurately propel a missile towards a target that was forty yards away. Obviously taken with a combination of the plaintiff's stubbornness, as well as his honesty and sense of humour, the S.F.A. upheld the appeal and Stein's famous impatience with those who were careless in their work, espe-cially referees, had won him the day once again.

The height of irony was that even if Stein regarded his right leg, in a playing sense, as being no better than an artificial limb, it was as a result of a severe injury to his right ankle that he had to finish as a player in August, 1955. Only months before he had led Celtic to another Scottish Cup final after beating a disorientated Airdrie side at Hampden in the semi

Putting players through hoops was what Stein was good at, according to his former pupils. A youthful David Hay looks none the worse.

finals. Doug Baillie, now a popular sports writer, was still at school then but played as the opposing centre half to Stein in front of over 70,000 people.

'I was just a raw boy then but I can remember throwing myself at a corner kick from Ian McMillan as Jock Stein came out to meet the ball as well. Blood spurted everywhere but big Jock got to his feet, lifted me up and said, 'That's us blood brothers now,' and then dropped me back down on the seat of my pants once again!'

There was no such humour when Stein met with his accident against Rangers at Celtic Park. Even at the age of 33, Jock resisted the temptation to accept his lot and retire gracefully to reflect on a good innings. He had not believed that he was achieving the maximum satisfaction out of the game until Celtic signed him as a full-time professional. Up until then he had only played the game as a means to earn money to supplement his wages for working underground, and his reluctance to concede his time was up took him all the way to Harley

Street specialists. The damage done was so bad, however, that Jock walked with a pronounced limp from then until the time of his death thirty years later.

It was Bob Kelly's decision to keep him at Celtic Park as coach to the reserve team, and there were palpably obvious signs of improved planning with regard to the training of the younger players. Celtic's first team were in the early stages of a seven-year-long barren run that would last until the mid-sixties, when Stein returned as manager. In his first season as reserve team coach, however, they won the Second Eleven Championship, securing the title at Dens Park. Willie Thornton was then manager of Dundee and could sense that his first impression of Stein as one of the shrewdest tacticians and disciplinarians he had come across had been absolutely correct. The opportunity for advancement in management did not exist at Celtic Park for Stein at that time, though, and he knew he would have to move away. There were rumours that he could be offered the vacant Partick Thistle job, but this was given to Willie Thornton instead and Stein survived a short leet to become the manager of Dunfermline.

With that heavy irony which always seems to punctuate a good story, his first match in charge was against Celtic, and his previously fierce allegiance was put to one side, if not entirely diluted, as Dunfermline won 3-2. It would become a depressingly familiar pattern so far as Celtic supporters were concerned, culminating in Stein leading the Fifers to a Scottish Cup final win, after a replay at that, in 1961 which caused traditionalists to question the old beliefs, such as the infallibility of the Old Firm when given a second chance.

In April, 1964, however, Stein left East End Park a much better place than he had found it and moved on to take control of Hibs, quickly winning the club their first honour of any description in ten years by defeating Aberdeen in the final of the short-lived Summer Cup. The fact that neither Celtic nor Rangers took part and that Hearts withdrew in midstream because of a prior commitment to a tour of the United States was irrelevant. Stein had proved beyond all reasonable doubt

May, 1978, Billy McNeill shakes hands with Desmond White on the day he succeeded Stein as Celtic manager. Privately, Stein is unable to settle and his days at Celtic Park are numbered.

that he had the necessary knowledge and the luck that even the greatest of managers need to keep on winning. Celtic, having gone seven unrewarding years, knew it was time for historic decisions to be made, and Bob Kelly was not one to shirk his responsibilities when such a job had to be carried out for the good of his club.

Not since the moves in the last years of the nineteenth century to have Celtic adopt a sectarian policy of signing only players of a Catholic persuasion had their religious origins and practices been brought so sharply into focus. All of Stein's family associations from Lanarkshire were vehemently Protestant, and Celtic had never employed a manager who did not come from the Catholic community, the ethnic minority in Scotland for whom the club had become standard bearers. As much as he had enjoyed wearing a green and white hooped jersey, Stein relished even more weaving an unexpected line through the fabric of Scottish society. More than the social order would change with his appointment, too.

With his last game in charge of Hibs, Stein had eliminated Rangers from the Scottish Cup. The tilt in Scottish football's balance of power began with that act and ended in April, 1965 when Stein's Celtic beat Dunfermline in the Cup final at Hampden and he set out on the road that led him to the equivalent of canonisation in the eyes of the supporters.

Celtic totally dominated Scottish football for the next ten years, with the finest day in the club's history coming on the 25th of May, 1967 in Lisbon where Stein outfoxed the previously feared manager of Inter Milan, Helenio Herrerra, as Celtic became the first British club to win the European Cup. The Liverpool manager, Bill Shankly, had articulated the innermost feelings of all Celtic's suddenly dumbstruck following that day when he strode across the team's dressing room, oblivious to the players there, and with his hand extended proclaimed, 'John, you're immortal!' The pressures of management eventually began to take their toll, however, and in 1973 heart trouble had led to Stein being hospitalised. In 1975, while returning from a family holiday in Minorca, his Mercedes was involved in an horrific crash with a Peugeot travelling on the wrong side of the A74 near Dumfries. Though he came back to manage the club once again, and to win a League and Cup double, Stein took a long time to get over the effects of that accident.

'You don't see all the damage,' he had confided to his players, explaining to them that the traumatic consequences of such an event are not purely physical. His last season as manager was also one of unqualified misery. Failing in the league through lack of proper expenditure on the team, Celtic finished fifth and did not even qualify for a place in Europe. The Scottish Cup ended ignominiously, too, with Celtic going out, after a replay, to a First Division side, Kilmarnock. The League

Cup went into extra time and then into Rangers' hands, but it was the European Cup which fully exposed Celtic's inability to protect their own, and Stein's, reputation.

The aggregate score of 4-2 against S.W.W. Innsbruck read like an obituary, and the night of the second leg in Austria saw the habitual sufferer from insomnia, Stein, take a sleeping pill and retire to his room, mentally preparing himself for his time at Celtic Park coming to an end. He was never blamed by the Celtic support, who would, tragically, be able to give full rein to what they really thought of him in 1985 on the occasion of his death. First of all, though, a crowd of 60,000 turned up for his testimonial match against Liverpool in August 1978 after Stein had made way for Billy McNeill to take over as manager. Unable to reconcile himself to the idea of the commercial post the club had set aside for him, Stein became manager of Leeds United but lasted only forty-four days at Elland Road before the pull of an invite to take over the Scottish national side, mixed in with misgivings about his move to England, became too strong to be resisted.

It was on the night of September 10 at Ninian Park in Cardiff that Jock Stein died of heart failure at the end of the drawn match with Wales which virtually guaranteed Scotland a place in their second, consecutive World Cup finals under him. He had looked desperately unwell sitting on the bench at the touchline and uncharacteristically detached when Davie Cooper's belated penalty kick gave Stein's team the result they needed.

Stein's funeral was at Linn Crematorium on the South side of Glasgow on Friday, September 13. A crowd of ten thousand men, women and children lined the route as the funeral cor-tège passed by. Bereft of a marked grave or any form of shrine to him, they went the following day to the one place where they knew they could best pay tribute to his memory, Celtic Park. The crowd of 39,450 turned up not just to see Celtic play Aberdeen but to honour him with their silence for one minute and then to chant his name in an emotional out-pouring at the ground of the club he above all had made famous.

Even through his years away from the club, Stein had frequently returned to Celtic Park to walk around and re-immerse himself in everything that was happening there. The devastated fan who had wanted to express himself on the passing of the man who was ultimately respected by people of all denominations and even by those who knew nothing about football but were simply taken by his presence, knew which was the best address to deliver his floral mark of respect. The accompanying card left outside the door of 95 Kerrydale Street read, 'Jock — heroes live forever.'

### INTERNATIONAL CAPS

N.B. Jock Stein did not win a full cap for Scotland.

1954

| Apr. | English League | (a) | 0-4 |
|------|----------------|-----|-----|

This was his only representative honour, a Scottish League cap.

CHAPTER FOUR

# *Jimmy Johnstone*

Jock Stein, when asked once to isolate what he considered to be his greatest single achievement in his time as manager of Celtic, ignored the winning of the European Cup for the first time by a British club and the world record-equalling performance of gaining nine league championship titles in succession and said in all sincerity that his best work had been done in keeping Jimmy Johnstone in the game at the highest level five years longer than he would have done if left to his own devices.

A supreme entertainer as well as a lavishly gifted and dangerous player, too much of the public's perception of John-

'Jinky' Jimmy Johnstone:
a supreme entertainer.

stone is taken up with the complex image of a man who had a pathological fear of flying but no qualms at all about drifting out into the Firth of Clyde in the dead of night in a small boat with no oars. Realising that his uncut diamond of a player was imprisoned by the vagaries of his own personality, however, Stein's paternal influence over Johnstone represented energy well spent, and desperately needed, too, when it is considered how little the player could give of himself on the field when not within the sphere of the manager's control and whenever he left Celtic Park.

A total of twenty-four Scotland caps and the candid admission that he cheated by not being able to give of his best once he had joined Sheffield United in the prematurely declining years of his career is as regrettable as Johnstone's decade of accomplishment at Celtic Park was a thrilling source of enjoyment to all who watched him play during that time.

In order to fully understand Jimmy Johnstone, though, it is first necessary to be aware of how so many demons could fight for space within such a small frame. Deeply insecure as a child because of his lack of height, the primary schoolboy from Uddingston was never to forget being humiliated by a teacher in front of a classroom of his peers.

Troubled by a skin illness that caused him to have his head shaved and required him to go to St. Columba's wearing a balaclava to cover up his total baldness, Jimmy was ordered to remove the protective garment and suffer the derision of his fellow pupils. The experience of running from there all the way home had a profound and lasting effect on the youngest of five children. Thereafter permanently unsure of himself physically and scholastically, Jimmy Johnstone learned to articulate himself on the football pitch.

If there are those who would say that a talent as deep and as rich as his was had to be God-given, he himself would only accept that as being partly true. As a youngster he had gone as part of the St. John's Boys Guild team to play a match in Manchester and can vividly recall sitting watching a television in his boarding house that was showing a film clip of the 1953 F.A. Cup final in which the Blackpool winger Stanley Matthews had

The fickle finger of fate was usually to be found pointing Johnstone's way.

immortalised himself by the way in which he fashioned the win over Bolton Wanderers.

'At that precise moment, I knew that was what I wanted to be, but I was not so young I failed to appreciate that it would take practical work to complement the ability I had been born with.'

Mastery of the ball, for him, had to be accompanied by pace and perfect balance. At the nearby ground of the junior club, Thorniewood United, Johnstone would develop both facets on his own for long hours every night.

'I had read that Stanley Matthews would wear heavy brogue shoes on his way to play in any match so that he would feel as light as a feather when he actually changed into his football boots. I borrowed huge pit boots from my father and raced up and down the heaviest parts of the pitch in a way that definitely made me quicker on a Saturday. I would also change into my stocking soles and walk along the top of the tubular fencing that surrounded the pitch, bending and turning to achieve better balance.'

Whatever he could do to improve himself as an athlete, Jimmy always needed the re-assurance of others that he was doing the right thing, however, and but for the arrival of Jock Stein as manager at Celtic Park in 1965 it is not inconceivable that he could have drifted away from the club altogether. He had fully expected a free transfer at the end of his first season there but was given out to the junior side, Blantyre Celtic, as a way of building up his confidence and hardening him to the rigours of the game.

On his return as a full-time player, Johnstone had come into the side at that inauspicious period in the club's fortunes when there were occasional embarrassments and continual failure to make the most of what was the nucleus of what turned out to be the most distinguished side in the club's entire history. His first-team debut in 1963 had been as part of a side beaten igno-miniously by six clear goals at Kilmarnock and for two years there was an immovable feeling of not really being wanted by the club, with its inevitable side effect of creating ever-dimin-ishing confidence. There was only ever going to be one man who could manipulate him, and the process of rehabilitating Jimmy Johnstone began before Stein had officially joined Celtic.

'I was having one of my periodic spells in the reserve team when we played Hibs, who were then managed by big Jock. At half time I had gone into the bathroom when he came wander-ing in at my back and started criticising me for letting myself go to the extent that I was not making it impossible for Celtic to leave me out of the first team and for not even putting enough into the game that night. After telling me to get out on to the park and show the crowd what I could do in the second half, I scored a hat-trick against his side.'

'Without football I would have amounted to nothing and but for him I would have had no sense of direction in my career, either. Jock never wasted words with you , but whatever he said was always the soundest advice you were ever likely to get.'

'For a long time I honestly thought he didn't like me, too, but I know now that he looked out for me more than any other player because he regarded me so highly. Since his death, I have met his wife, Jean, on more than one occasion and she is always telling me about the soft spot that Jock had for me. I take it as a compliment that he could describe his greatest achievement as keeping me in the game because it shows he felt I was worth saving in the first place.'

It must have been the breathtaking virtuosity of Johnstone that kept the manager going, though, because the player had an uncanny attraction to trouble on and off the field at the same time, coupled with a major drawback for someone inex-orably drawn to controversy, the unfailing knack of getting caught. Only Jimmy Johnstone, for instance, could have chosen Armistice Day to get sent off for the first time in his pro-fessional career at the start of a record that would show a total of seven dismissals in all.

'I often think, though, that I might not have been the player I was without that level of aggression in me. There is no point in glorifying the trouble I got into, however. I regret all of it now and the minute after I had become involved in a scuffle, like the first time I was sent off with Ian Cowan of Partick Thistle, in 1963, I had calmed down and was full of remorse. I needed the high tension level, though, to bring out the best in me.'

Once he had properly established himself in Jock Stein's team and embarked on the road that led him to nine league championship winners medals, four for the Scottish Cup and five in the League Cup as well as a European Cup Winners Cup medal, the debate would start as to which was Johnstone's finest game among the many he won for Celtic. The European Cup-tie against Red Star of Belgrade in 1968 is popularly thought to be the most obvious example of what Jimmy John-stone was all about, with its peculiar background that had Jock Stein promising him he need not put his detestation for flying to the test once again if he could create an aggregate lead extravagant enough for Celtic to feel comfortable in the second leg.

Johnstone dismantled the Yugoslavs on his own and even scored twice as well as laying on three other goals in a mesmeric performance that had him leave the field in tears shouting to no-one in particular, 'I don't need tae go' over and over again. The player himself, on the other hand, would pick an ordinary league game that took place against Dundee United a year later at Celtic Park as his favourite memory and encapsulation of the full extent of his capabilities.

'Celtic won 7-2 and I gave the crowd what they wanted to see. My adrenalin always started to flow at a furious rate when I felt in the mood and I could sense the crowd were willing me on. I would beat three or four players that night and then double back and beat them all again. That was what excited me more than scoring goals and I touched heights then that were exhilarating even for me. Late in the game I hit the post, too, but I never did manage to get a goal. That didn't bother me, though, because I had laid on most of the ones we did get and if I had walked round the whole of the Dundee United team that night I would have got a bigger thrill rolling the ball along the line for somebody else to score. I can always remember Davie Wilson, who had left Rangers for Dundee United, standing at the mouth of the tunnel waiting for me after the final whistle just to congratulate me on my performance, and the respect of a fellow professional like that meant a lot to me.'

Johnstone's Old Firm contemporary was Willie Henderson and it was, indirectly, their rivalry that got Jimmy's international career off to a bad start from which it never properly recovered. In what was only his sixth appearance for Scotland, against Wales at Hampden in 1967, the highly sensitive Johnstone was barracked by supporters at what is traditionally the 'Rangers End' of the stadium, who then took to chanting the name of Henderson.

'Rightly or wrongly, I came to the conclusion that these people did not want to see me in a Scotland jersey and, to be perfectly honest, I was never all that bothered about playing for the national side, anyway.'

'If ever I was asked how I would like to be remembered in the game that would be simply as Jimmy Johnstone, Celtic player; all the rest you can keep so far as I am concerned.'

Jimmy joins in celebrating Celtic's 4-0 Scottish Cup victory over their great rivals, Rangers, in 1969.

His ambivalent attitude towards representing his country also had its roots in the congenital shyness that made him feel uneasy at the start in the company of more worldly men like Denis Law and Billy Bremner, but it was two separate incidents before matches against England that attracted the maximum publicity and ensured only a fragile peace thereafter when he was included in a Scotland pool. In February, 1968, only three months after his demoralising experience at Hampden, the Scotland squad of which Jimmy was a member travelled to

Largs for training, but when the side was announced the name of Johnstone had been left out.

A practice match was then arranged for the team against Celtic at a junior ground in the seaside town. It was Walter Macrae, later to become the manager of Kilmarnock but who was then assistant to the national coach, Bobby Brown, who approached Johnstone in the militaristic manner that was his trademark and asked him to act as linesman in that match. The response to what was more of an order than a request was predictably volcanic and required all of Brown's powers of diplomacy to quieten tempers and allow the player a comparatively low-key withdrawal from the match.

Months later, following Johnstone's decision to absent himself from the Scotland squad before another match with England, this time at Wembley, when he disembarked from a train in Edinburgh's Waverley Station and went home because of illness, Jock Stein delivered a stinging public rebuke to the player he normally protected.

'Bobby Brown obviously needs players he can depend upon and Jimmy Johnstone is not in that category,' he said.

What could safely be called a mercurial career in a Scotland context continued in that vein until his last appearance on his country's behalf, against Spain at Hampden in November, 1974, and was always of greater value to all branches of the media than it was to the player himself or the various managers who had to contend with him and his problems. His notoriety peaked with the infamous sailing incident at Largs, when a nocturnal notion for a boat trip, which had developed on the way back to the Scotland team's hotel from a night's carousing in a local pub, brought down a farcical curtain on the proceedings. It is sad to relate that a player of Johnstone's universal renown never played in the World Cup finals when such a stage might have been created for extravagant talents such as his. Jimmy lost his final opportunity, the 1974 World Cup in West Germany, as a consequence of an assortment of misadventures like his sudden attraction to the sea.

A pre-World Cup warm-up against Belgium and Norway saw Johnstone, who scored Scotland's only goal in the defeat by the Belgians and then get the winner in Oslo, involved in another much publicised spot of revelry on licensed premises that put paid to his prospects of taking part in the finals as his career at both international and club level slipped inexorably towards an undistinguished close. Peculiarly, his last cap for Scotland came only eight months before the patience of Jock Stein was finally exhausted and, exasperated by the failure of his attempts to rehabilitate his incorrigible player, the manager made it known that Johnstone was to be given a free transfer from Celtic Park.

'The full impact of what I had lost never struck me until I was physically handed my P45 form by one of the office staff at the ground. I burst into tears at the sight of it and got out of the place as fast as I could because I was heartbroken.'

For all that his career was in comparative tatters, Johnstone retained a firm belief in his own worth on the open market, and for that reason he rejected the chance to join the then fledgling New York Cosmos, who were looking for a suitably grandiose name to enhance their image in the eyes of an American public waiting to be coaxed into stadia on that continent as the game tried to take off there in a serious fashion.

'They came to me before Pele, remember, but for a ten-week season I was offered £12,000 and no firm idea of what was to happen when that time was up, so I turned them down and asked for more money. My reasoning was that if they were looking for instant status for their club the terms were not in keeping with the job that had to be done and, although I never did get the money, I think my point was proved to be a valid one when they went for Pele instead and paid him a fortune for going to the States.'

Johnstone eventually did make it to America, but to join the far less celebrated San Jose Earthquakes. He got to play on the same field as the legendary Brazilian as well, when their two sides met in the Yankee Stadium.

'The game finished in a penalty shoot-out, but before then I had the ultimate satisfaction of having Pele come over to me at the end of regulation time and make that gesture of joining a digit to the thumb on one hand that signified he felt my display had been spot on. He said what sounded like 'Magnificent' in his broken English and that moment will live with me for ever. Without wishing to sound irreverent, it was the footballer's equivalent of being blessed by the Pope! It was always the same with me, I needed to feel the necessity to play at my peak. When the European Cup-winning side of 1967 played Real Madrid shortly after that triumph in what was the testimonial match for Alfredo di Stefano inside the Bernebeau Stadium, we beat them by the only goal of the game and when the Celtic team had been reduced to ten men after Bertie Auld was sent off. I was very conscious then of appearing in one of the game's great theatres if you like.'

'In the dressing room beforehand, I can remember sitting there, looking around me and thinking about all of the times Real had won the European Cup, how they had actually been given the original trophy to keep and of all the wonderful play- ers, not only from that side, who must have graced their pitch. After that, Jimmy Johnstone from Uddingston could hardly wait to get out there and show what he could do.'

Whether it was playing an ersatz form of the game in the United States or taking his experience and ability to Sheffield United after that, such an uplifting feeling would only return once at each place for Johnstone. After the respectful meeting with Pele, the next time was when playing on the opposite side from another of the genuinely great players of his era, George Best.

'After leaving Celtic Park the game itself no longer held a thrill for me. I have to be totally honest and admit that I cheated the public at Sheffield United. I went through the motions for the two years of my contract at Bramall Lane. It was a nice place to live but the club itself appeared to be only a stopping- off point for people who had no ambition to do anything but look forward to their next move. I fell into the trap and allowed myself to become complacent. The total absence of the lift I used to get from the crowd in the 'Jungle' at Celtic Park didn't help me, either, and there is only one game that stands out in my mind. Sheffield United played Fulham at Craven Cottage in London and Georgie was on the other side. I can't even

The 'Lisbon Lions' before the historic European Cup defeat of
Inter Milan, 2-1. Jimmy is fourth from right.

Jimmy, front row, second from left, in a staff photocall,
season 1968-69.

remember the score that day, but it was an unimportant incidental, in any case. The fact that he was on the park was enough to get me interested. He went through his party pieces, I went through mine and the crowd loved it, that was all that mattered.'

The party was well and truly over, though, and in the years that went between then and his retirement there came the long and meandering road home for Jimmy Johnstone.

A short stay with Dundee in season 1977/78 was ended with a move to the League of Ireland side, Shelbourne. Even more improbably, Elgin City became the next refuge for Jimmy before, in 1980, his playing life turned full cycle when he was reinstated to the junior ranks with Blantyre Celtic, the club where Celtic had sent him to learn his trade and where he ended up playing beside those who were in primary school when he was being celebrated throughout Europe.

It was during David Hay's brief stay as manager of Celtic that Jimmy went back to the club to coach their youth team when, it is said, part of the youngsters' eduction was trying to get the ball off their tutor on training nights. The flirtation with that side of the game was short-lived and ended with internal strife being at the core of Johnstone's decision to divorce himself from football altogether. There was never any likelihood of him being tempted to try management after he had fallen out with Celtic's chief scout and others, but not Hay.

'For one thing, if I ever work for any football club again it will be Celtic and no other because there is still no place that matters as much to me. I couldn't possibly be a manager, though, since I know without having to prove it to myself that I do not have the necessary temperament for the job. I could never tell a boy that he was getting a free transfer, for example. Basically, I am only interested in working with a ball at my feet. Even now when I watch a good game on television I have an overwhelming urge to go out into the street or the local park and have a kick about. I don't, though, because I have this fear of people laughing at the man in his forties who thinks he can be the way he used to be. I can still appreciate the entertainers, though, like Joe Miller at Celtic Park. I know comparisons are drawn between us by some supporters and I can see the resemblance. Joe is one I would get out of the armchair to go to watch.'

The time-consuming demands of business, though, prevent Jimmy from attending too many matches in person these days. Employed as a salesman on behalf of a firm who deal in satellite dishes for picking up foreign television, the one who was once the talk of Europe now enables others to buy a glimpse of continental football. It is debatable if any of his customers will see anything on their screens that will surpass the excitement that Jimmy Johnstone could generate on the days and nights when he felt the urge to step out of himself and express in deeds what he felt was relevant about the game.

### FULL INTERNATIONAL CAPS

| 1964 | | | |
|---|---|---|---|
| Oct. | Wales | (a) | 2-3 |
| Oct. | Finland | (h) | 3-1 |
| 1966 | | | |
| Apr. | England | (h) | 3-4 |
| Oct. | Wales | (a) | 1-1 |
| 1967 | | | |
| May | U.S.S.R. | (h) | 0-2 |
| Nov. | Wales | (h) | 3-2 |
| 1968 | | | |
| Nov. | Austria | (h) | 2-1 |
| 1969 | | | |
| Apr. | W. Germany | (h) | 1-1 |
| Oct. | W. Germany | (a) | 2-3 |
| 1970 | | | |
| May | England | (h) | 0-0 |
| Nov. | Denmark | (h) | 1-0 |
| 1971 | | | |
| May | England | (a) | 1-3 |
| Nov. | Belgium | (h) | 1-0 |
| Oct. | Portugal | (h) | 2-1 |
| Dec. | Holland | (a) | 1-2 |
| 1972 | | | |
| May | N. Ireland | (h) | 2-0 |
| May | England | (h) | 0-1 |
| 1974 | | | |
| May | Wales | (h) | 2-0 |
| May | England | (h) | 2-0 |
| June | Belgium | (a) | 1-2 |
| June | Norway | (a) | 2-1 |
| Oct. | E. Germany | (h) | 3-0 |
| Nov. | Spain | (h) | 1-2 |

## CHAPTER FIVE

# *Bobby Murdoch*

Celtic's entry into the sixties was endured more than enjoyed by their supporters, who viewed the team's collective state as the various members would a touch of madness in the family. The affection was congenital and undying but it was better not to speak about the cause of their suffering and try to remember them as they were. Derangement on the park was brought about by the loss of the influential players like Evans, Peacock and Stein on top of the process of natural wastage that had accounted for Tully and the other, more brittle talents. The residue floated aimlessly from one mishap to another, preparing

May 25, 1967, Bobby Murdoch and Jock Stein on the night Celtic won the European Cup and the 'Lisbon Lions' were born.

at one time for a European tie by scoring four goals in the first fifteen minutes of a league game against Third Lanark at Celtic Park and then losing four themselves before the end to snatch an eccentric draw from the jaws of an extravagant victory. A veil would have needed to be drawn over the outcome of almost every Old Firm game of the period, and the internal bickering during the interval of one comprehensive defeat at Ibrox meant that one of the club's genuinely gifted contributors, Paddy Crerand, never played again for Celtic and was eventually sold to Manchester United. Soon after, the disaffection of the supporters could no longer be discreetly hidden and there was a public demonstration outside the ground after Queen of the South drew with Celtic in a League Cup tie. It was the only point Queen of the South would get out of six sectional games and the unseemly scenes as the dissidents wailed for the removal of the Celtic chairman, Bob Kelly, were redolent of the mourners turning on the pall bearers as the funeral procession passed by. Out of this generally inauspicious environment, and that one game in particular, grew up one half of the European Cup-winning team, and among them Bobby Murdoch.

His affection for Celtic was heartfelt, and in an age when there still existed that breed who would play for the jersey, putting remuneration for wearing the colours into second place, Murdoch could have been considered the perfect example of the type in that it actually cost him money he could ill afford to go on to the club's staff.

The oldest of four boys from Rutherglen, on the outskirts of Glasgow, Murdoch had been exceptionally gifted from an early age. He can recall playing a trial for the Lanarkshire junior club, Carluke Rovers, when he was fourteen, which might not have been considered sufficient maturity to watch some of what went on at that level of the game from the comparative safety of the terracing. Before he had left Our Lady's High School in Motherwell, Bobby's obvious potential had earned him the offer of training facilities with the highly respected senior team the manager, Bobby Ancell, had constructed on stylish lines at Fir Park. When, in 1960, a leisurely game of bowls with his father in the local public park had been interrupted by Jimmy

McGrory and Jock Stein with the specific purpose of inviting him to work under Celtic's guidance instead, however, there was no equivocation, as the basic arithmetic of his decision would fully illustrate.

'As soon as I had written to Mr Ancell saying I was going to Celtic, a letter I felt I had to send out of courtesy, I received almost by return of post an offer of £8 a week to stay with Motherwell.'

His wage at Celtic Park would be £3 a week as a part-timer, making Bobby's move an incongruous one for a boy whose family were no different from those around them in that any extra money could readily be put to good use, and not on the provision of smoked salmon for the common table, either. Interestingly for one who would come to be regarded as one of the mainstays of the Celtic side in their greatest years, Murdoch elected to be semi-professional and take a job as a sheet metal worker in Springfield Road, adjacent to the ground, ensuring that the combination of hard work by day and physical exertion at night resulted in the memory of his recreational hours being dominated by waking up in an assortment of cinemas to the tune of the national anthem playing.

'I had no way of knowing at that age if there was a living to be made purely by playing football, and although my father was a great Celtic man I felt I had to make up my wages for my mother, who received an unbroken pay packet every week I spent living under her roof.'

The unpredictable nature of the game is always best emphasised by recounting the misfortunes of those who have been struck down by debilitating injury while either on the threshold of greatness or at the peak of their powers. Bobby Murdoch, unknown to the vast majority of those who followed his career with growing admiration, played for ten of the thirteen years he spent with Celtic suffering from a chronically damaged right ankle that had to be bathed in hot water and carefully bandaged before every game he took part in, and which has left him today with a legacy of pain that antibiotics will not deaden. Even in Celtic's moment of supreme achievement, the winning of the European Cup final against Inter

Murdoch: A Celtic man who believed in playing for the jersey.

Milan in Lisbon on the 25th of May, 1987, Murdoch's ankle was swathed in bandages and his movement severely restricted.

'If you look again at the television recordings of that game and, with the benefit of video machinery, freeze any close up of me you will see that my right ankle is almost twice the size of the left. I don't think I kicked the ball with my right foot any more than five times over the course of the entire ninety minutes' play, and I was playing at right half. Even the shot I had at goal, which was deflected by Stevie Chalmers to give us the winner and the trophy, was struck with my left foot.'

The damage, unsuspected till now, had been done when the then eighteen-year-old Murdoch, a year after making his league debut for Celtic, had sustained horrific injury to the ankle ligaments in a match against Hearts.

'I can still recall Gordon Marshall, who was Hearts' goal-keeper that day, coming off his line and shouting frantically to the referee, 'I never touched him, honest to God I didn't.' He was telling the truth, too, because I had hurt myself. It was a rainy day and I had worn long studs to give myself a better grip on the greasy surface, but in stretching to connect with a cross as Gordon came out to meet me I had caught my studs on the grass and put the full weight of my body on the ankle ligaments, causing them to bend backwards. The pain was excruciating and I had to be helped off the field in tears. Years later I used the ankle as a barometer of how important a game was to Jock Stein when he became manager of Celtic. If he didn't come in to the treatment room while I was lying there and ask Neil Mochan, who was then our trainer, how I was progressing that meant big Jock knew he could get by without me. However, if he came in and simply said, 'I suppose he'll be all right for Saturday,' I knew that was my signal to get off the table and go to work. The years of practice at bandaging the ankle for myself had made me able to go out on to the park, no matter the importance of the occasion, without any worries, subconscious or otherwise, about making things worse.'

Before Stein had arrived to practise man management, Murdoch had resolved to play through the discomfort, in any case, in order to make his mark on a struggling team. There

was only one occasion on which even his willingness to with-
stand physical pain and forebear in the face of the psychological pummeling that came with a Celtic jersey at that time led to
a weakened resolve. One month after the demonstration outside the ground following the draw with Queen of the South in
August 1963, Murdoch had still to re-appear in the first team.
When the scapegoat was then excluded from the travelling
party bound for Switzerland and the European Cup Winners
Cup tie with Basle, he decided to ask for a transfer. Celtic were
only in Europe because the League champions, Rangers, had
also humiliated them in the Scottish Cup final of the season
before, during the replay of which Murdoch had featured in the
fortieth different forward permutation used by Jimmy
McGrory.

All the frustration of being part of a young side lacking in
direction engulfed him and if it had not been for the calming
influence of his family, who had their relative's welfare as well as
the club's at heart, an invaluable part of a Celtic side on the
verge of immortality would have been lost for the price of a
stamp.

'Deep down I had complete respect for our chairman, Bob
Kelly, and what he was trying to do. He was a fair man who knew
as much about the game as anyone who was at Celtic Park in
1963. He had decided the only way back from obscurity was to
rear our own players and he would persevere even in the face
of public discontent because he knew, instinctively, that he was
correct.'

It was with the arrival of Stein, at Kelly's request, in 1965 that
Murdoch, like his team-mates, Billy McNeill, John Clark,
Tommy Gemmell, Jimmy Johnstone and Bobby Lennox, was
put out of his misery and given a reason to look forward again
without worrying what might befall them next.

'The quickest way to sum up the difference Jock made is to
say that it was as if we had been sitting in a darkened room and
he came in and switched on the light.'

Within forty-six days of coming Stein had led Celtic to the
Scottish Cup, their first trophy in eight years, by beating Dunfermline in the final. The following season Celtic won the

League championship for the first time since Stein had captained the club twelve years earlier. By then the manager had given Murdoch a new position in the side, moving him from inside right to right half and with responsibility for taking control of the ball and making full use of it with a passing ability that was telescopic in its accuracy. It was a function for which he was so naturally suited that Bobby Lennox could say of him, 'For me, he was the best player in the team that became known as the Lisbon Lions. People talk about great players and the phrase is used very loosely. Bobby Murdoch, though, was a really great player; it was an education to watch him.'

After the European Cup had been won and Celtic had taken part in the infamous World Club Championship against the discredited winners, Racing Club of Argentina, another South American side, Boca Juniors, had inquired about the possibility of buying Murdoch from Celtic. Stein, who was a great loss to the world of espionage in the way that he could make an art out of being furtive when he wanted to be, had never told the player of this exotic opportunity until he was absolutely certain it would not come off, which would be a recurring theme while Murdoch played in a way that gained him respect at home and on the continent. In 1969 he was named Scotland's Player of the Year by the Scottish Football Writers' Association, the third winner to come from Celtic in the four years of that accolade's existence.

'Funnily enough, the award came after I had suffered more trouble with the ankle injury that I was still trying to keep a secret. I was carried off before half time in a League international at Dalymount Park in Dublin and missed the next four matches for Celtic. I'll always remember being sent a letter by a Celtic supporter at that time who called me for everything for allowing myself to be hurt at a critical stage of the season while wearing a Scotland jersey. So far as he was concerned, Celtic paid my wages and that should have meant not risking myself while wearing dark blue. If only he had known that I was technically unfit to play every week of that season. The irony was I came back after that break feeling refreshed, and if I had to pick one game that gained me the writers' acclaim it would be the first

For ten years Bobby hid the secret of a badly damaged ankle.

leg of the European Cup tie with Red Star Belgrade at Celtic Park. This is usually recalled as the night Jimmy Johnstone had one of his most unforgettable games for the club but I scored the opening goal and laid on the last one for wee Jimmy in our 5-1 win.'

By now, though, Europe had become a recognisably tougher place for Celtic and those of their supporters who thought that by winning the Champions Cup in 1967 at the first attempt it was always going to be as easy as that.

There was one more final to come, though, and on the way to it, in 1970, Celtic became the first British club side to beat an Italian team over two legs in the European Cup. Passaola, the coach of the vanquished Fiorentina, described the strength of Murdoch's contribution by saying, 'He is the Papa of the team; the rest are the sons around him.' Five days before the final itself, when Celtic met, and failed to beat, Feyenoord in Milan's

San Siro stadium, the legendary Lisbon Lions had played in a league match that was a stage-managed farewell to eleven men who would never come together again on the park. Clyde were summarily taken apart by six clear goals, and if the feeling among those watching was that things would never be quite the same again, Bobby Murdoch was not long in finding out the truth of those words.

Another possible move from Celtic to Everton had been avoided, again by the simple expedient of Stein not telling Murdoch that Harry Catterick, the manager at Goodison Park, had wanted him. Because no business could be done in Glasgow, Everton had bought Allan Ball from Blackpool instead.

'By the time I got to hear about any of this Jock's exaplanation to me was that he had told Harry Catterick I had wanted to spend all of my playing career with Celtic.'

By then this was becoming a presumptuous statement for the manager to make without first consulting his player. In any brief résumé of Bobby Murdoch's career, the average follower would say that, at Celtic Park, he was latterly beset by weight problems. He would not deny that such difficulties existed but Murdoch would maintain to this day that they were exaggerated.

'At the end of 1969 Jock suggested I should go away to Lief's Nature Cure Centre in Tring, in Hertfordshire, for what was called a twelve-day conditioning course. In effect I was there to lose a stone in weight, which I did, but not through a tortuous diet, more because of what I would call a regime of sensible eating.'

'In fact, I came back on schedule to play my part in winning the League Cup from St. Johnstone. I honestly felt that the manager made more of the problem than was necessary at times.'

Regardless of any personal and subjective interpretation of the player's physical condition, the incontestable truth is that from then on Bobby Murdoch was, at the age of only 25, never again the same player for Celtic. The stay in Tring cured him of certain habits but could not curb every urge. Like a fighter struggling to make the weight, he would occasionally come back and rekindle the memory of what he had once been but

The penultimate triumph. Celtic celebrate their draw with
Dukla Prague and entry into the European Cup Final.

there would also be relapses. Extra weight also put additional strain on joints that compounded the problem. But for Murdoch's unfortunate metabolism, which meant the dietary routine of a jockey if he was paying attention and the obvious presence of unmanageable weight when he was being careless, he might have left Celtic even earlier than he did, however, and missed out on the remaining distinctions that were still to come his way. His difficulty in stabilising his weight certainly cost him the opportunity to finish his career with Manchester United.

'When Tommy Docherty was manager of Scotland he had suddenly asked to have me brought into the squad for the Home International Series. I had been out of training for just over a week by then and was starting to enjoy the close season away from Celtic Park, so that was already long enough to make sure I was in no fit state to be playing at that level. I told Jock Stein as much when he called me at home with the Doc's message but he insisted I come into the ground and let him be the judge of what was best. When I got to Celtic Park, though, I telephoned Tommy Docherty and told him the same story. I had played against England in particular once before when I was in something less than peak condition and we had lost heavily at Wembley so I did not want to go through that experience again. The telephone conversation ended abruptly, though, with the Doc hanging up on me and big Jock looking unhappy.'

'The only reason I tell the story is that some time later Jock called me into the board room at Celic Park, which was an unusual thing in itself, and told me to sit down.'

'I have a bit of a shock for you,' he said. 'Manchester United want to buy you. Frank O'Farrell's been on the phone.'

'And I have got a bit of a shock for you. I'm going,' I told Jock. He wasn't exactly pleased and told me to go home and talk it over with my wife. My mind was made up, though. And then came an unbelievable sequence of events. Frank O'Farrell was sacked and his successor, I don't need to tell you, was Tommy Docherty, which effectively blocked the road between Glasgow and Manchester for good so far as I was concerned.'

In 1973, Bobby signed a new two-year contract with a two-year option that Celtic could pick up if they wanted and, in spite of almost leaving, was content to see out the remainder of his days with the club. Only six months of the agreement had elapsed, however, when he played his last-ever game for Celtic, against Arbroath on tiny Gayfield Park on August 29, 1973. It was a League Cup tie played under the experimental rules of the time which meant that there was no off-side between the eighteen-yard lines that had been extended out to the touch-lines on either side. For Stein, this was the kind of game that required younger players of Kenny Dalglish's stamina and made Murdoch redundant. That arrangement was made formal on September 17 when Jack Charlton took Bobby to Middlesbrough on a free transfer.

'I remember going to the Old Firm game at Ibrox, a fixture I had always detested for the way the tension strangled the creativity out of the players involved, and taking a last look at the team. Jimmy Johnstone, who had been one of my best pals when that side let its hair down away from the game, scored the winning goal and I went to a family party that night as the only one who knew I would be leaving Glasgow.'

'When I walked out of Celtic Park two days later as an ex-Celtic player I couldn't have looked back to see the place, in any case, for the tears in my eyes.'

Longevity was given to Murdoch's career with a deeper-lying role at Ayresome Park that relied heavily on his artistic use of the ball and less on his mobility when not in possession, giving him a total of nine satisfactory years in England. In that time he assisted in the development of the younger players round about him, including an Edinburgh teenager whose career needed re-directing after a false start with Spurs. His name was Graeme Souness. During that time Bobby also became a fully qualified coach and ultimately took over the managership of Middlesbrough with an apparently hopeful new road stretching before him. His club, however, showed a distressing willingness to sell its best players to all and sundry, but mainly their direct competitors, and there came the inevitable consequences. Relegation and the easy option of replacing the manager who had gone down to the Second Division with the club followed. Today, after a brief time spent coaching Celtic's youth team, Bobby Murdoch has no official connection with the game and is rarely, if ever, a spectator at matches anywhere.

Celtic's club history will judge him as one of the finest players ever to wear their hooped jersey, though, even if there will be a lingering sense of regret that he left Glasgow at what should have been the peak of his career. More recently, there have been problems with illness, and while being grateful for the memory of what Murdoch achieved wearing the number four shorts there is also an eagerness now to see him restored to good health and fully able to enjoy whatever is in store for him in the future.

## FULL INTERNATIONAL CAPS

### 1965

| | | | |
|---|---|---|---|
| Nov. | Italy | (h) | 1-0 |
| Nov. | Wales | (h) | 4-1 |
| Dec. | Italy | (a) | 0-3 |

### 1966

| | | | |
|---|---|---|---|
| Apr. | England | (h) | 3-4 |
| Nov. | N. Ireland | (h) | 2-1 |

### 1967

| | | | |
|---|---|---|---|
| Oct. | N. Ireland | (a) | 0-1 |

### 1968

| | | | |
|---|---|---|---|
| Dec. | Cyprus | (a) | 5-0 |

### 1969

| | | | |
|---|---|---|---|
| Apr. | W. Germany | (h) | 1-1 |
| May | Wales | (a) | 5-3 |
| May | N. Ireland | (h) | 1-1 |
| May | England | (a) | 1-4 |
| Nov. | Austria | (a) | 0-2 |

The homecoming. McNeill and Murdoch lead the team on to the pitch
at Celtic Park with the European Cup.

## CHAPTER SIX

# *Billy McNeill*

On the night of May 25, 1987, the twentieth anniversary of Celtic's win over Inter Milan in the European Cup final, in a bar on the South side of Glasgow called Heraghty's, a capacity crowd assembled to commemorate the club's achievement in the old-fashioned way while at the same time lending a whole new meaning to the phrase about drinking in the atmosphere. There were sufficient numbers claustrophobically gathered inside the small premises to have impromptu stewards deployed at the only entrance to prevent further over-crowding, and the only outward movement allowed was the occa-

Billy McNeill: Back in his rightful place as Celtic manager in time for the club's centenary year.

sional release of those physically unable to make a path across the mass of humanity that separated them from the public conveniences. The escapees were permitted to use the facilities at the adjacent public house, where the staff absent-mindedly wiped glasses into a state of transparent cleanliness to the undisturbed ticking of a clock while wondering what all the fuss was about inside the competition's premises next door.

The climax of the evening's entertainment in Heraghty's was the showing of the full ninety minutes at the Estadio Nacional, complete with accompanying sound effects from the watching throng as they gave a fair impression of supporters who had never watched this particular spectacle before when they could, in fact, have mouthed the entire commentary from memory as if it were film dialogue because of their familiarity with the work.

At that point where the game is over and the Celtic captain eventually makes his way to the ornate dais where he becomes the first British player to accept that trophy, looking at the same time the living embodiment of his nickname of Caesar, the door of Heraghty's opened as far as it could to admit Billy McNeill in person. If the entrance was Messianic, the response was fittingly reverential as well. Where there had been congestion, there suddenly appeared space for the man whose qualities of leadership on and off the park had an inspirational effect on those who followed his career as Celtic player and manager.

For the previous four years, McNeill had been like deposed royalty in exile, banished to England after an internal row with his directors at Celtic Park. His return, though, had long been hoped for by his adherents, and two days after he had gladly joined in with the faithful rank and file in a mood of nostalgic celebration there was an outbreak of topical festivity when Billy McNeill was re-appointed Celtic manager.

There are certain mental images of McNeill frozen in the minds of those who see him as Celtic's figurehead in a natural line of succession starting from Jock Stein and for whom the club's centenary year would have been hopelessly incomplete unless he had re-assumed the manager's office in time for that milestone in their history. The first picture etched on the con-sciousness is of the blonde-haired figure rising above his own team-mate, Bobby Lennox, to head in the winning goal that gave Celtic the Scottish Cup against Dunfermline in 1965 and breathed new life into a side that had been ailing for the previ-ous eight years through stultifying non-achievement. The sec-ond, permanent recollection is the appropriately dramatic vision of McNeill showing the European Cup to his team's fol-lowers in the amphitheatre that was the Estadio Nacional.

His departure from the club after the blood-letting of 1983 had created a spontaneous period of mourning, during which those unable to come to terms with their grief had alluded to him as 'Our manager in Manchester' in a form of coded short-hand while he was in charge of Manchester City. If Celtic are a metaphor for life for some people, Billy McNeill has always been looked upon as the head of a family unit by a support who can readily appreciate that, essentially, he is no different from them in the depth of his affection for the club.

The most influential player to represent Celtic in the second half of this century is also blessed with undeniable charisma and an ability to be an articulate spokesman on the club's behalf and his own. Appearing on a B.B.C. television pro-gramme of political discussion shortly after his return to Glas-gow in 1987, McNeill was described by the presenter in her introductory remarks as a man who loved Celtic more than his own family. If there was an obvious inclination towards hyper-bole in order to establish credentials, it is true to say McNeill would never disguise his feelings for Celtic as an institution.

'In actual fact, I had been taken to see Celtic play for the first time by my Aunt Grace. My father was a professional soldier who did not always have the time to do that and I have honestly always felt lucky in life, in that all I ever wanted to do was play for Celtic and then become their manager, both of which I have achieved.'

McNeill had been signed by Celtic but was out on loan to the Lanarkshire junior team, Blantyre Victoria, when the club won the League Cup final against Rangers in 1957. From then until

Hail, Caesar! McNeill goes out on top as a Celtic player following the defeat of Airdrie in the 1975 Scottish Cup Final.

his moment of acclaim in the mid-sixties at Hampden, McNeill grew to become a regular Scottish internationalist and a highly respected centre half in a club side that had a glorious past but apparently nothing very much to look forward to. It would not be exaggerating at all to venture the possibility that, but for the Scottish Cup being won against Dunfermline, McNeill would have gone from Celtic Park in 1965, and not out of disaffection, either, so much as an overwhelming feeling of personal frustration.

'I was twenty-five years old by then and had never won anything of note in the game. It is at a time like that a player comes to think on a purely personal level and I had plenty of clubs, like Manchester United, Leeds United and, above all, Spurs whispering in my ear that I might be more fulfilled joining them.'

'The funny thing was, I always felt Celtic were fated to win the Scottish Cup that season regardless of anything, but it was the arrival of Jock Stein as manager shortly before we did that had the most significant influence on my decision to stay, and after we had beaten Dunfermline I would have to say that the next ten years of my playing life were highly pleasurable indeed.'

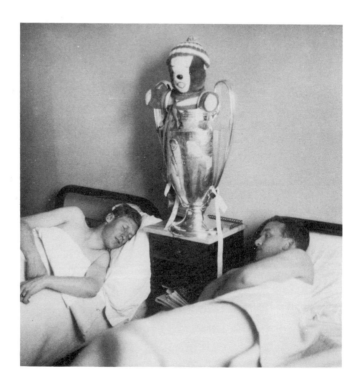

Dreaming of what was to come: McNeill (left), John Clark and an unidentified bodyguard for the European Cup.

The fruits of his labours: McNeill's winners medals alone are thought to constitute a world record for one man.

A sense of pre-destiny where Celtic are concerned is a theme to which McNeill persistently returns when analysing the club and what it means to him and those who support them. For McNeill, there had consistently been a fairy-tale element about Celtic, and after Stein had been installed in the seat of authority there were always going to be more happy endings than any other kind.

'I can remember talking to Jimmy Gordon, who is now the

managing director of Radio Clyde, in 1966 about that aspect of the club. He was directing the filming of the *Celtic Story,* which was to capture the progress of the team throughout the 1966-67 season as well as give a historical account of the team's origins, and Jimmy told me he instinctively felt the same way about them. As it turned out, of course, the cameras recorded us winning every domestic competition we entered and came over with us to Lisbon for the grand finale.'

To carry the feeling of pre-ordination to its logical conclusion would be to suggest, then, that, as some supporters believe, what was done then could never be repeated because the eleven players who defeated Inter Milan represented a blend of youth and experience along with a favourable mix of playing attitudes that the fates are unlikely to throw together again twice in the lifetime of the same organisation, no matter their flair for living out a fairytale existence.

'That team might not have stayed together at all had they been born into this modern era of freedom of contract, but those were less sophisticated days and I believe the players then got more enjoyment out of playing the game and gave a lot more, too, because they paid a lot less attention to what they were getting paid.'

'Perhaps it was all meant to happen for Celtic when you take into account things like Jock Stein buying Willie Wallace from Hearts so that he could play up front beside Joe McBride, only to find, unfortunately, that Joe injures himself so badly he misses half of the season and Stevie Chalmers, who took his place, gets the winning goal in Lisbon.'

McNeill was at his imperious and assertive best during that European campaign, having the title of Caesar bestowed upon him for the way in which he led from the front on a journey that started in Zürich and went through France (v Nantes), Yugoslavia (v Vodjvodina Novi Sad) and Czechoslovakia (Dukla Prague) before the coach to the Italian side, Helenio Herrera, was forced to concede that Celtic's win over Inter Milan was a 'Victory for sport'. McNeill's goal in the last minute of the second leg of the Quarter Final tie against Vodjvodina in Glasgow had carried the side through on a 2-1 aggregate, and his com-

August, 1987. A hero's return; Billy McNeill takes his seat in the stand at Celtic Park and his place in the hearts of the fans.

manding display in the air in what was a purely defensive stance that had guaranteed safe passage into the final itself was the highlight of Celtic's defiance of the Czech army side, Dukla, on their own ground.

In the seven years that followed, McNeill would also be able to claim the commendable distinction for a centre half of having scored goals in three separate Scottish Cup finals, a statistic that any forward might be pleased to have against his name. As well as that, McNeill can look back on being the first man ever awarded the title of Scotland's Player of the Year by his peers (in 1965) and having the letters M.B.E. put after his name for services to the sport in 1974. In a career that spanned seventeen seasons in all at Celtic Park, Billy played over 800 times for the club, and his haul of twenty-three winners medals in major competitions is thought to constitute a world record. There were, in the interests of accuracy, nine League Championship medals, seven in the Scottish Cup out of a record twelve appearances in Hampden finals and six

League Cup winners medals as well as his treasured European Cup medal that is today worn by his wife, Liz, as a piece of jewellery.

There are, though, no visible traces of memorabilia in the McNeills' Glasgow household that would give away the identity of his profession to the unsuspecting visitor.

'I try to be immersed in the club when I am at Celtic Park and a husband and father when I come home. The caps, medals and souvenir jerseys are all in cardboard boxes somewhere.'

And yet McNeill is an obvious sentimentalist. Celtic are, to his way of thinking, the underdogs in their own city and he protects them from harm with a ferocious dedication. As a player he had been the same, detesting defeat and developing a ruthless competitive edge that only once in eighteen years caused him to be sent off.

'Players in the sixties and seventies had a higher regard for one another. I worry about the lack of respect modern-day players give each other when I see them deliberately trying to get their fellow professionals into bother on the park.'

McNeill can not easily tolerate any criticism of his club that he feels is unwarranted or unfounded, and yet for someone so opinionated he will hint at having been led into retiring from the game as a player in 1975. As he had started off the greatest era in the club's history by going up to accept the Scottish Cup a decade earlier, so Billy spent the last day of his working life in a hooped jersey on the winners rostrum at Hampden with the same trophy held above his head after Celtic had beaten Airdrie. By his own admission, abdication from the leadership of the team was at least two years before he should have gone from the game he had graced.

'Sometimes you listen to people telling you the time is right to go and you grow into the idea that getting out on top like that at Hampden is the only way to bow out. I realised less than a year after I had gone, though, that I had made a big mistake. There was a business to be looked after by then, however, and I started to watch Celtic play, home and away, like an ordinary supporter with my pals and I derived a lot of enjoyment from that.'

Being an impassive onlooker was never McNeill's style,

though, and after a brief flirtation with journalism as a television analyst of the game he was initially coaxed into coaching Celtic Boys Club. In April, 1977, Billy took charge of Clyde and at Shawfield he took a practical grounding in management. By the start of the following season he had applied for, and got, the job of succeeding Ally McLeod as manager of Aberdeen.

'A lot of people mention only the more colourful side of Ally's personality but I have a lot of respect for him and what he did on a business level at Pittodrie. Aberdeen had always been a well organised, efficiently run place and he kept that up, making it easy for his successor to come in and get on with handling the team.'

Under McNeill, Aberdeen reached the final of the Scottish Cup and finished second in the Premier League Championship in what was to be his only season there. On both occasions McNeill had been runner-up to Rangers. When, in May, 1978, he was offered the job of replacing Jock Stein as manager of Celtic there was much that needed to be done at Celtic Park but, equally, there was never any doubt that McNeill would find it impossible to resist the call for help.

Needing assistance himself as Celtic finished the first half of their league programme in the bottom half of the table, McNeill found it in the shape of a ten-week break caused by an excessively bad winter, emerging from the hiatus with a side able to collect thirty points out of a possible thirty-six in the concluding phase and able to close their run by dipping into the apparently bottomless pit of fairytale endings and defeating Rangers 4-2 with only ten men on the park and having been a goal down with less than twenty-five minutes to play at Celtic Park. In his first tour of duty, McNeill won three League Championships in total as well as both the League Cup and Scottish Cup.

If there is a period of Celtic's modern history that the supporters would like to erase from their minds, it would be the events leading up to McNeill's enforced departure from the club in June, 1983. A well-publicised piece of thinking out loud, to the effect that it came as a surprise to him that his managerial efforts had not been seen fit to merit the offer of a contract with the club, was misinterpreted as a demand for better terms, and there then followed a statement from the board at Celtic Park that McNeill's request for a wage rise, which had never existed, had been denied. For a man as proud as McNeill, the pre-emptive action of his employers was tanta-mount to showing him the door that led to the street outside the ground, and within a matter of days, to the dismay of those who looked on powerless to act, he was appointed manager of Manchester City. It had often been said privately that Billy McNeill led a colour supplement-style existence with an idyllic family life, a prosperous business and the gratitude of those who idolised him for the way he ran Celtic. The manner of his leaving Glasgow, though, was consistent with the unsavoury list of headlines that had heralded his violent disagreement with a journalist in a London hotel on the eve of Celtic's depar-ture for a European Cup tie, the costly downfall of his business, and the acrimonious exchange of private details relative to McNeill's earlier financial arrangements that embarrassed those who believed the entire affair to be a blot on the club's good name.

When the subject of that period is raised now, McNeill's dis-quiet is obvious.

'It was a bad time for me, and one that caused me personal problems. For the first year I was away, I began to experience the feeling of losing my regard for Celtic. I knew I still had the moral support of the fans because it was not uncommon for whole busloads of them to turn up at Maine Road on a Satur-day to see Manchester City play, and I had also heard how the supporters were making their feelings known about what hap-pened through the medium of radio and newspaper corres-pondence columns. It was still not a time I would care to live through again, however.'

There were other, more public outpourings on his behalf, as well. A visit to the 1985 Scottish Cup final, when Celtic met Dundee United in the one hundredth climax to that competi-tion and McNeill was one of several former winning captains ceremonially presented to the crowd beforehand, inspired an ovation that could not be ignored in high places. Another symbolic outburst greeted him on the night the Affiliation of Registered Celtic Supporters Clubs held a dinner to mark the twentieth anniversary of Lisbon. Seven hundred fans gave McNeill a frenzied reception in the presence of Celtic directors at a Renfrewshire hotel which prompted days of high activity behind the scenes at board level.

'I was supposed to go home to England the day after that dinner but my very good friend, and former team-mate, Mike Jackson, invited me to stay on at his house. We went to Heraghty's the following night without saying anything beforehand because it was near his flat and word of mouth had suggested it was going to be a special evening. The morning after I got a call asking me to meet Jack McGinn, who had become Celtic's chairman in my absence, and I was eventually offered my job back.'

The significance of all that took place was not lost on McNeill. The club's centenary year would have been a hurtful time for him had he not been delivered back into Celtic's hands. The disagreement with the board would not have allowed him to be part of the celebrations, while his non-appearance would have ruined the occasion for others.

At the time, McNeill's attitude was to speak of being a 'changed man', moulded by his experiences, good and bad, in the South, and the period since then has convinced him he was correct in that assessment. Like Jock Stein, McNeill's relations with the representatives of the media can be abrasive and characterised by a withering stare or a chilling word or two of rebuke, but basically they are less volcanic than before. He is in greater control of himself and assured that the course he is taking with the club is the right one. While the reconstruction of Celtic Park's facade has been taking place outside his office window, McNeill would admit to thriving on the turmoil that has gone on inside.

'Since coming home to the park, I have felt time going faster than at any other stage in my life, and I can say that as someone whose family had grown up before I knew it when I was in this job before.'

The burden of carrying supporters' expectations is not intimidating for him, either. McNeill described anonymity as being nice but accepts that the manager of Celtic must live with the responsibility of caring for the aspirations of supporters who refer to the team as 'us'. For that reason it is his intention to make the club more accessible to the man in the street than any other of a comparable size.

'I mean it when I say that, no matter what Celtic may achieve, they will always be the underdogs in Glasgow. We could never spend the money Rangers do, for instance, but we will work in other ways to bring about success our own way.'

The winning of the Premier League Championship was the complete vindication of McNeill's playing and fiscal policies. While the club record for buying new players was created by him with the signing of Frank McAvennie, McNeill resisted the clamour to bring back Charlie Nicholas. The former Celtic player's lukewarm response to the notion of re-joining McNeill made certain of that.

Even though McNeill knew there was scepticism over his decision to spend £850,000 on the older McAvennie, the player himself repaid his manager's faith in him and won over the supporters with goals and industry. Billy Stark, taken from Aberdeen for £75,000, and Chris Morris, an unknown from Sheffield Wednesday, represented managerial shrewdness of a high order, and the swiftness with which Joe Miller was purchased and produced in front of an adoring public reassured everyone that the fortunes of the club were in the most capable pair of hands there were in a Celtic context. The re-signing of Paul McStay on a long-term contract and the improved standard of play perceptible in someone like Peter Grant confirmed that feeling.

McNeill was wounded by the savage criticism that followed him back to Glasgow after his time with Manchester City and Aston Villa, but the fairytale ending he assumes is Celtic's copyright remains in good working order, and that is why the things that are Caesar's, pride and respect, were handed back to him.

McNeill's winning goal against Dunfermline in the Scottish Cup Final of
1965 ended eight barren years and led to a decade of plenty.

## FULL INTERNATIONAL CAPS

**1961**

| | | | |
|---|---|---|---|
| Apr. | England | (a) | 3-9 |
| May | Eire | (h) | 4-1 |
| May | Eire | (a) | 3-0 |
| May | Czechoslovakia | (a) | 0-4 |
| Sept. | Czechoslovakia | (h) | 3-2 |
| Oct. | N. Ireland | (a) | 6-1 |

**1962**

| | | | |
|---|---|---|---|
| Apr. | England | (h) | 2-0 |
| May | Uruguay | (h) | 2-3 |

**1963**

| | | | |
|---|---|---|---|
| June | Eire | (a) | 0-1 |
| June | Spain | (a) | 2-6 |
| Nov. | Wales | (h) | 2-1 |

**1964**

| | | | |
|---|---|---|---|
| Apr. | England | (h) | 1-0 |
| May | W. Germany | (a) | 2-2 |

**1965**

| | | | |
|---|---|---|---|
| Apr. | England | (a) | 2-2 |
| May | Spain | (h) | 0-0 |
| May | Poland | (a) | 1-1 |
| May | Finland | (a) | 2-1 |
| Oct. | N. Ireland | (a) | 2-3 |
| Oct. | Poland | (h) | 1-2 |

**1967**

| | | | |
|---|---|---|---|
| May | U.S.S.R. | (h) | 0-2 |

**1968**

| | | | |
|---|---|---|---|
| Feb. | England | (h) | 1-1 |
| Dec. | Cyprus | (a) | 5-0 |

**1969**

| | | | |
|---|---|---|---|
| May | Wales | (a) | 5-3 |
| May | England | (a) | 1-4 |
| May | Cyprus | (h) | 8-0 |
| Oct. | W. Germany | (a) | 2-3 |

**1972**

| | | | |
|---|---|---|---|
| May | N. Ireland | (h) | 2-0 |
| May | Wales | (h) | 1-0 |
| May | England | (h) | 0-1 |

CHAPTER SEVEN

# *Kenny Dalglish*

It is arguable if there has been a more accomplished player to represent Celtic in the entire history of the club than Kenny Dalglish. Laid end to end, his achievements at Celtic Park show how lengthy was the journey in a relatively short time on their behalf of an extraordinary talent fully entitled to be described as World class. In 328 competitive games, Dalglish scored a total of 199 goals for Celtic, winning five league Championship medals along with four for the Scottish Cup and another one in the League Cup. Dalglish is also the joint holder of the record for having scored most international goals for Scotland, a distinction he shares with Denis Law, and is the first man ever to

Kenny Dalglish: A rare moment of relaxation in the midst of years of accomplishment at Celtic Park.

get one hundred caps for his country. As well as that, Kenny Dalglish is the only player ever to have scored one hundred League goals for one club in the country of his birth as well as another one hundred in the English League. For such a distinguished career at Celtic Park and Liverpool, he was made a Freeman of the City of Glasgow in 1985 and since then he has proved that, devastating though he may have been as a player, Kenny Dalglish was also capable of making the transition into a staggeringly successful manager by assuming control at Anfield in a way that made the job look far easier than it really is in those surroundings.

All of this is merely to establish credentials on behalf of a person who aroused strong feelings among Celtic supporters, emotions which, by their ultimately volatile nature, emphasised the kind of effect he had on them. Within the space of six months in 1987, Dalglish appeared twice at Celtic Park, once in the colours of his own club, Liverpool, in aid of Tommy Burns' testimonial year, the other turned out in Celtic's hooped jersey.

The mere promise of that nostalgic sight was enough to encourage a crowd of well over forty thousand people to come out on a raw December night for the match that was Davie Provan's benefit on his enforced retiral from the game. Dalglish was warmly, even ecstatically, received on both occasions.

There may have been some who attended both those games, however, who had taken their children to see the Celtic legend that was Kenny Dalglish but could have owned up to taking part in a more hostile form of reception ten years earlier for the same man. It was, up until then, a common courtesy that former Celtic players were never verbally abused from the terracing when they returned to the ground where they had once enhanced the jersey. An embarrassing exception was made in the case of Dalglish when Celtic met Liverpool in the showpiece game that would formally recognise, and recompense, Jock Stein for all he had done for the club, not the least of which was nurturing the talent of the young Dalglish himself.

In August, 1978, Kenny Dalglish was roundly booed from the start of the game until the very end, the bitterness of the supporters at his decision to leave Celtic a year before still

199 goals for Celtic were not come by without having to survive special treatment.

deep enough for them to revile someone who had for a time carried the team on his back with the help of Danny McGrain when dark passages in their progress were being negotiated. Kenny will tell anyone now that the experience of that night did not affect him and that he knew beforehand it was coming, anyway. The supporters' grapevine in Glasgow, on occasions flawlessly accurate in its information, had warned of a public demonstration to underline the resentment, and Dalglish's family connections in the licensing trade had picked up some of the messages across the city.

Acknowledging Dalglish's diplomacy and still close affinity with Celtic, it is for the observer to state, therefore, that what happened to him that night was an act of betrayal on the part of some Celtic supporters. Their feelings of being deserted by the player were totally unfounded. Dalglish could, in fact, have moved on a year earlier than he did but stayed on out of a sense of loyalty to the club who had taught him the game, as well as an affection for Celtic that had been cultivated from the day when he was to be found running round his own home in Glasgow frantically trying to remove photographs of his favourite Rangers players from the walls before they became a source of embarrassment when Sean Fallon came to sign him.

Kenneth Mathieson Dalglish is as Glasgow as Sauchiehall Street and was, consequently, as prone as the next man, or boy, to being caught up in the one thing that actually divides the city, namely the vexed question of 'Who do you support?' His emotional attachments lay unequivocally with Rangers and were sufficiently powerful, in fact, for Kenny to have reservations about Celtic's offer to train with them. It is the kind of congenital condition that has an effect on the everyday lives of supporters in a place where garden fencing can be painted in a colour scheme that freely advertises which half of the historic divide resides at that address, and where supporters will not go to a game at the other side's ground because they would not feel ideologically sound after giving their admission over in a way that would be akin to sponsoring the Bader-Meinhof gang.

Having said that, Dalglish played for the ironically named

Dalglish scores against Hearts — later he would break the hearts of those who idolised him.

Glasgow United, where he fell victim to a flaw in the system with regard to supporting, or playing for, one half of the Old Firm being looked upon as a person's birthright. It was generally accepted in the circles in which Glasgow United moved that Dalglish would become a Rangers player one day by a process of logical progression. Nobody from Ibrox scouting staff ever came forward to actually formalise the arrangement, though, and, being sensible enough not to let tribal instincts get in the way of ambition, Dalglish took up Celtic's offer, albeit without remembering to get rid of the last vestiges of his allegiance to Rangers. When Sean Fallon, then the club's assistant manager, arrived to complete Celtic's coup, at a house almost on the doorstep of Ibrox to compound the feeling of felonious intent, there were so many photographs of people in blue jerseys the distracted boy eventually had to give up the chase and stood almost luminous with embarrassment while watching Celtic's representative see the funny side of it. The thought of what the fact of Dalglish's signing for Celtic might do for the humour of some not far away might have increased Fallon's tolerance level as well.

It was the time of Celtic's European Cup win in Lisbon, too, and the afterglow of the team's achievement against Inter Milan could still be felt as warmly as the summer sunshine that greeted Dalglish's arrival for his first day of training at Celtic Park in July, 1967. Kenny will go out of his way now to state that everything he has achieved in the game had its basis in those early days when Jock Stein, Sean Fallon and Willie Fernie took the bones of his talent and gave it flesh and blood by working morning and afternoon on Dalglish and his contemporaries. Together they were fashioned into a reserve team that could be compared to their peers at that level only in the sense that they all had two arms and two legs.

Needing to beat Partick Thistle's second eleven by seven clear goals at one time in order to gain entry to the later stages of the reserve League Cup, Celtic scored six times in each half to provide one of those results that always looks like a misprint. There could be no mistaking Dalglish's ability, though, and among the many landmarks in his career will always be an early appearance in the first team in a testimonial match for Frank Beattie of Kilmarnock. Kenny scored six of Celtic's seven goals that evening and the moment of his permanent elevation to the side could no longer be ignored.

Conversationally, Kenny Dalglish has the disconcerting habit of making any question, no matter how carefully thought out and painstakingly constructed it is with the specific intention of eliciting a lengthy and candid response, seem bland and worthy only of the type of response that can make a person wish he had never opened his mouth in the first place. For instance, Dalglish's introduction to the first team on a regular basis was also the occasion of his first Old Firm derby at Ibrox on August 14, 1971, the opening day of that particular league season. With twenty minutes to go and Celtic already a goal ahead, they were awarded a penalty kick that stood every chance, if converted, of finishing the game prematurely and in their favour.

Such is the way of these matches, however, that failure to take advantage of such a gift can invite the other side to behave as if they have just been given additional oxygen and lead to a

A characteristic pose for Dalglish — a familiar position for opposing goal-keepers.

hectic finish. Nevertheless, it was Dalglish who was entrusted with the job of instigating the former course of action. Amid the accompanying braying that is customary at such moments in an Old Firm context, especially when the lungs of the on-lookers are being fully exhaled for the first time after the close season, the youngster could be seen to interrupt his approach to the ball as it waited like a ticking bomb on the spot and begin adjusting his boots.

Could this have been, one wondered, a hastily contrived ploy, designed to lower the pulse rate of someone who was entitled to have been in a high adrenalin state?

'No. I was tying my lace,' he says pragmatically, giving the impression of wondering what this introspective analysis is all about. Needless to say, Dalglish scored from the penalty kick, of course. Within four months of that day at Ibrox, too, Kenny had won the first of his 102 caps for Scotland. It was a phenomenal rate of progress and one that introduced him to Sandy Jardine, then of Rangers, now the co-manager of Hearts. Jardine has no doubts at all about Dalglish's place in the contemporary history of Scottish football.

'In the last twenty-five years there have been only a few World class players to have represented Scotland. Denis Law was one, obviously, Billy Bremner and Danny McGrain were others and Kenny Dalglish was indisputably in that company as well. He was a gifted player who made up for any deficiencies in his game with a mind that allowed him to be a step ahead of everybody else on the park at any given time. Kenny was not the paciest player I have ever come across but before he had even gathered the ball he knew where he was going to put it next and that is a tremendous advantage to have on your side.'

In one of the first marriages between the commercial world and football at that time, Jardine and Dalglish were formed into a pair by a personal agent and indulged in the usual activities to capitalise on their popularity, including the release of a record that at least gave the public a sign of human frailty on the part of both men. Jardine was offered an insight into Dalglish's character that few were able to get, therefore, and his summation is a respectful one.

'I know that Kenny would occasionally find the public appearances we did a painful experience. He was neither a professional speaker nor a stand-up entertainer, he was a football player, pure and simple. Kenny does possess a strong sense of humour, though, as well as a single-mindedness that some people can mistake for aloofness. He does not suffer fools gladly but, as one who knows how difficult club management can be, I can have nothing but respect for what he has achieved at Liverpool in such a short space of time. It is all very well saying he had a lot of money to spend on players, but those millions of pounds have to be invested wisely in the first place. How can you argue, too, with someone who has won the

Dalglish and Sandy Jardine release their record — but prove that we all make mistakes!

League and Cup double in his first season in charge of any club?'

Dalglish's single-mindedness could on occasion be translated into a ruthless streak on the park and Jardine would recall him, their business association notwithstanding, as someone who could 'dig a bit', which is the players' definition of a person who has the ability to receive and the power to give back again with interest, especially in the course of the Old Firm confrontation. With that practised gift of being able to summarise years of involvement in a ritualistic spectacle that has at one time or another attracted the attention of a universal audience and is known, albeit vaingloriously, as the greatest club game in the world, Dalglish would call the Celtic-Rangers matches 'All right, so long as you win.'

They are, though, among the highlights of his ten years at Celtic Park, possibly because he would react well to the fact that, in his participation in those games, Dalglish was on the

winning side twelve times out of nineteen matches. This is consistent with a thread that runs through Dalglish's career, one of
high achievement that hints at a state of near perfection, but
there were minor disappointments along the way. At club and
international level the year of 1976 would be punctuated by
negative reasons for remembering that particular time in his
life. When Scotland played Wales at Hampden in August of
that year, Dalglish was in line to win his 34th full international
cap in succession, a feat that would have seen him surpass the
record he then held jointly with George Young of Rangers. In
spite of injuries to a couple of players that would have allowed
for Dalglish's appearance as a substitute, and regardless of the
fact that the possible creation of a new milestone had been a
conversation piece in the build-up to the match, Scotland's
then manager, Willie Ormond, left him on the bench con-
sumed only by a sense of frustration.

As his international team-mate and close friend, Sandy Jardine, would acknowledge, it was a peculiarity of Dalglish's
Scotland career up until then that he had never fully convinced
the demanding public at Hampden that he could in fact repro-
duce his form for Celtic in a dark blue jersey.

'The point about it was that Kenny would not push himself
while in the company of those Scotland players who were
regarded as the elder statesmen of the side at that time. At Celtic Park he would have been familiar with everyone on a daily
basis but when it came to the business of the irregular international get-togethers Kenny was inclined to say nothing and
think a lot.'

Dalglish, for all that he was capable of stunning virtuosity,
was the perfect team member and it may have been that which
swayed him towards Liverpool when the time finally came for
him to remove himself from Celtic Park instead of going to the
repository for the individually blessed that was Manchester
United's Old Trafford.

Ten wins in the major domestic competitions in only six
years of regular first-team football had been satisfying but Celtic's inability to make a mark in Europe in the decade that followed the club's domination of that theatre of operation was a

It could be a word association test, what do you think when you hear the name, Dalglish?

source of extreme irritation to Dalglish. Twelve months before he joined Liverpool, Kenny had contemplated leaving Glasgow but, for once in his life, he was prevented from seeing through something he had wanted to do by an overwhelming feeling of disloyalty leading to disquiet.

'Big Jock Stein was in hospital at the time recovering from the car crash that almost killed him and Sean Fallon was doing his best to keep things running smoothly at Celtic Park. Billy McNeill had only retired from the playing side a year before as well and, all things considered, I felt I was letting Celtic down at a time when they needed me most, so I signed a new, one-year contract instead of asking for a transfer. When that was up, though, I told Mr Stein that I still had the urge to try my luck elsewhere. He did succeed in getting me to sign a new agreement but only on the understanding that it was for Celtic's good in the short term and that, ultimately, they would let me go when the time was right.'

Dalglish had signed in order to be registered in time for the Scottish Cup final of 1977 against Rangers, and so as not to create an unsettling feeling of discord in the sensitive days leading up to such an important match. Celtic, with Dalglish as captain, won the final by the only goal of the game, scored by Andy Lynch, but it would be his last appearance for the first team. After a summer of speculation, culminating in Kenny's refusal to go with the side on their pre-season tour of Australia, he played in a reserve match against Stirling Albion and was not permitted to captain the team. Four days later, in a friendly match with Dunfermline at East End Park in front of a meagre crowd, Kenny bade his farewell to Celtic. Later on that same night, as midnight approached, Dalglish met with Jock Stein, Liverpool's manager, Bob Paisley, and the Anfield chairman, John Smith, inside a deserted Celtic Park. Within minutes he had agreed to sign for them.

'I know there were stories about Jock Stein supposedly asking me just before I went in for that meeting if there was any-thing he could do to make me stay at Celtic Park, but it never at any time had anything to do with money. Of course it was a ter-rific wrench to leave Celtic. One of the biggest thrills of my pro-fessional life is, was and always will be the first day I got off that number sixty-four corporation bus and reported for training along with Danny McGrain. Celtic educated me in the game and without that solid grounding I would not be where I am today. The whole crux of the matter, though, was that I had faith in my own ability as a player. I had to know, therefore, if I could make it somewhere else and I wanted that place to be England. What I did not want was to go through the rest of my life won-dering what might have been without putting myself to the test. If my transfer to Liverpool hadn't turned out to be a good move, then I would have gone back to Scotland again to pick up my career there once again.'

The transfer fee of £440,000 was a British record at the time but looks like grand larceny now when it is recalled how Dalglish more than adequately replaced Kevin Keegan and sparked off familiar scenes of public adoration in Liverpool by scoring five times in his first six league matches. The words of the then chairman of the Professional Footballers Association in England, Cliff Lloyd, to the effect that such a sum was 'Unfair on the player and bad for the game generally' were greeted with incredulity on Merseyside and complete scorn in Celtic's

Dalglish: the perfect team member, perfectly upset.

half of Glasgow, where a fund to pay twice that figure to have Dalglish back would have been over-subscribed.

Ironically, Liverpool could have had Kenny for nothing ten years earlier. He had played a trial for them as a fifteen-year-old, representing Liverpool's 'B' team against Southport 'A' in Division Two of the Lancashire League, but had suffered badly from homesickness, so much so that even the persuasive tongue of the legendary Bill Shankly had been unable to get him back down again.

There can be no doubt that this simple twist of fate was Celtic's good fortune for a decade, and hindsight has lent the supporters of the club a more appreciative view of all that Dalglish did for their team during that time. He is still an attender at some of Celtic's important matches when his managerial schedule allows and turned up to watch the team make sure of the Premier League championship in their Centenary year by defeating St. Mirren at Celtic Park. His upbringing in the game was at the feet of the club's role models, the Lisbon Lions, but even the members of that revered side would agree that they can not take all of the credit for nurturing the talent that was put to Celtic's use over a period of thrillingly sustained achievement.

Jimmy Johnstone would pay him this glowing tribute: 'If any youngster wants to model himself on a player, then Dalglish is the man. He is undoubtedly one of the modern-day greats. Kenny's attitude was always right — on and off the park. He had fantastic close control and the ability to turn on a sixpence. Like all top-class strikers, he knew where the target was and hit it regularly. Dalglish was also very courageous, a point which is often ignored when people talk about him. He took a lot of hefty knocks but jumped up and kept on playing. I've seen times when his leg was heavily strapped up but he wanted to play. He had a great appetite for football and that made him an extraordinary professional in my book.'

### FULL INTERNATIONAL CAPS

| | | | |
|---|---|---|---|
| **1971** | | | |
| Nov. | Belgium | (h) | 1-0 |
| Dec. | Holland | (a) | 1-2 |
| **1972** | | | |
| Oct. | Denmark | (a) | 4-1 |
| Nov. | Denmark | (h) | 2-0 |
| **1973** | | | |
| Feb. | England | (h) | 0-5 |
| May | Wales | (a) | 2-0 |
| May | N. Ireland | (h) | 1-2 |
| May | England | (a) | 0-1 |
| June | Switzerland | (a) | 0-1 |
| June | Brazil | (h) | 0-1 |
| Sept. | Czechoslovakia | (h) | 2-1 |
| Oct. | Czechoslovakia | (a) | 0-1 |
| Nov. | W. Germany | (h) | 1-1 |
| **1974** | | | |
| March | W. Germany | (a) | 1-2 |

| May   | N. Ireland     | (h) | 0·1 |
|-------|----------------|-----|-----|
| May   | Wales          | (h) | 2·0 |
| May   | England        | (h) | 2·0 |
| June  | Belgium        | (a) | 1·2 |
| June  | Belgium        | (a) | 1·2 |
| June  | Norway         | (a) | 2·1 |
| June  | Zaire          | (a) | 2·0 |
| June  | Brazil         | (a) | 0·0 |
| June  | Yugoslavia     |     | 1·1 |
| Oct.  | E. Germany     | (h) | 3·0 |
| Nov.  | Spain          | (h) | 1·2 |

**1975**

| Feb.  | Spain          | (a) | 1·1 |
|-------|----------------|-----|-----|
| April | Sweden         | (a) | 1·1 |
| May   | Portugal       | (h) | 1·0 |
| May   | Wales          | (a) | 2·2 |
| May   | N. Ireland     | (h) | 3·0 |
| May   | England        | (a) | 1·5 |
| June  | Rumania        | (a) | 1·1 |
| Sept. | Denmark        | (a) | 1·0 |
| Oct.  | Denmark        | (h) | 3·1 |
| Dec.  | Rumania        | (h) | 1·1 |

**1976**

| Apr.  | Switzerland    | (h) | 1·1 |
|-------|----------------|-----|-----|
| May   | N. Ireland     | (h) | 3·0 |
| May   | England        | (h) | 2·1 |
| Sept. | Finland        | (h) | 6·0 |
| Oct.  | Czechoslovakia | (a) | 0·2 |
| Nov.  | Wales          | (h) | 1·0 |

**1977**

| April | Sweden         | (h) | 3·1 |
|-------|----------------|-----|-----|
| May   | Wales          | (a) | 0·0 |
| June  | N. Ireland     | (h) | 3·0 |
| June  | England        | (a) | 2·1 |
| June  | Chile          | (a) | 4·2 |
| June  | Argentina      | (a) | 1·1 |
| June  | Brazil         | (a) | 0·2 |
| Sept. | E. Germany     | (a) | 0·1 |
| Sept. | Czecholovakia  | (h) | 3·1 |
| Oct.  | Wales          | (a) | 2·0 |

**1978**

| Feb.  | Bulgaria       | (h) | 2·1 |
|-------|----------------|-----|-----|
| May   | N. Ireland     | (h) | 1·1 |
| May   | Wales          | (h) | 1·1 |
| May   | England        | (h) | 0·1 |
| June  | Peru           | (a) | 1·3 |
| June  | Iran           | (a) | 1·1 |
| June  | Holland        | (a) | 3·2 |
| Sept. | Austria        | (a) | 2·3 |
| Oct.  | Norway         | (h) | 3·2 |
| Nov.  | Portugal       | (a) | 0·1 |

**1979**

| May   | Wales          | (a) | 3·0 |
|-------|----------------|-----|-----|

| May | N. Ireland | (h) | 1-0 |
| May | England | (a) | 1-3 |
| June | Argentina | (h) | 1-3 |
| June | Norway | (a) | 4-0 |
| Sept. | Peru | (h) | 1-1 |
| Oct. | Austria | (h) | 1-1 |
| Nov. | Belgium | (a) | 0-2 |
| Dec. | Belgium | (h) | 1-3 |

**1980**

| March | Portugal | (h) | 4-1 |
| May | N. Ireland | (a) | 0-1 |
| May | Wales | (h) | 1-0 |
| May | England | (h) | 0-2 |
| May | Poland | (a) | 0-1 |
| May | Hungary | (a) | 1-3 |
| Sept. | Sweden | (a) | 1-0 |
| Oct. | Portugal | (h) | 0-0 |

**1981**

| Feb. | Israel | (a) | 1-0 |
| Sept. | Sweden | (h) | 2-0 |
| Oct. | N. Ireland | (a) | 0-0 |
| Nov. | Portugal | (a) | 1-2 |

**1982**

| Feb. | Spain | (a) | 0-3 |
| March | Holland | (h) | 2-1 |
| April | N. Ireland | (a) | 1-1 |
| May | Wales | (h) | 1-0 |
| May | England | (h) | 0-1 |
| June | New Zealand | (a) | 5-2 |
| June | Brazil | (a) | 1-4 |
| Dec. | Belgium | (a) | 2-3 |

**1983**

| March | Switzerland | (h) | 2-2 |
| Sept. | Uruguay | (h) | 2-0 |
| Oct. | Belgium | (h) | 1-1 |
| Nov. | E. Germany | (a) | 1-2 |

**1984**

| Sept. | Yugoslavia | (h) | 6-1 |
| Oct. | Iceland | (h) | 3-0 |
| Nov. | Spain | (h) | 3-1 |

**1985**

| March | Wales | (h) | 0-1 |
| Oct. | E. Germany | (h) | 0-0 |
| Nov. | Australia | (h) | 2-0 |

**1986**

| March | Rumania | (h) | 3-0 |
| Sept. | Bulgaria | (h) | 0-0 |
| Nov. | Luxembourg | (h) | 3-0 |

## CHAPTER EIGHT

# *Danny McGrain*

It would be tragic if the memory of Danny McGrain's twenty years' distinguished service as a player with Celtic was to be tarnished, or even overshadowed, by the acrimonious nature of his departure from the club in 1987. There are those who would say that within the period dating from his first-team debut in 1970 until the mysterious ankle injury in 1977 that cost him a year out of his playing life, Danny could justifiably have laid claim to be the best full back in Europe during an era when that was a hard-earned distinction. What is incontestable is that his achievement in coming back after so long away and

Danny McGrain: the best in an era when that distinction was hard won.

adding nineteen full international caps for Scotland to the forty-three he had already won, thereby gaining him admission to the S.F.A.-inspired Hall of Fame as one of only eleven players to have represented their country on more than fifty occasions, isolated him as being a special type of individual as well as a notable talent. This was, after all, the player who had overcome a series of personal misfortunes in the form of diabetes, a fractured skull and a broken leg that would be regarded as mere incidentals along the way to making a name for himself.

It was at the end of Tommy Burns' Testimonial match, when Celtic played Liverpool in August, 1987, that the Celtic supporters publicly demonstrated their affection for McGrain amid the controversy over the manner in which he and the club's management had fallen out concerning the matter of his free transfer three months earlier. The disharmony that existed had come to the surface before the game had begun, when McGrain had rejected a request from the Celtic directorate to appear before the crowd in a stage-managed ceremony involving players past and present. A wave of emotional fervour at half-time, when he had been spotted in the stand by spectators who wanted a spontaneous happening of their own, had sent Danny scurrying into the bowels of the stadium, unwilling to draw attention away from the player who was the centre of attraction that afternoon. The groundswell of feeling that built up while Tommy Burns was taking a lap of honour at the end could not be ignored, however, and as the two players embraced on the field to a tumultuous welcome from the tens of thousands who had prompted their reconciliation, the public who had adored him said their respectful farewells to Danny McGrain.

'My unhappiness over the way in which my time with Celtic was formally brought to an end has not diminished in any way with the passing of time, but neither is it the first thing I think about when I open my eyes in the morning. The negative thoughts make up only 0.1% of my feelings as opposed to the 99.9% that is taken up by remembering all the good things about my years with Celtic.'

Danny McGrain was not brought up to support Celtic but, once there, he was easily absorbed into the club's attacking traditions. He would eventually replace Jim Craig, one of the Lisbon Lions, at right back in the first team as Jock Stein dismantled the side that was the embodiment of how Celtic, and those who followed them, saw the game as it should be played.

'Jim was a defender of outstanding quality and yet it was the more flamboyant nature of Tommy Gemmell, with his long, overlapping runs and that ferocious shot, that was the more talked about on the terracing. That was how it was, and always will be, at Celtic Park.'

In the early days, McGrain's energy had been boundless, so much so that Stein would have to tell him to cut down on the number of times he invaded the opposition's half of the field. His stamina had been built up as a boy on the acres of open space available in the sprawling Glasgow housing scheme of Drumchapel, where the duration of a bounce game with his fellow evacuees from the decaying tenements of the city centre would often be dictated by how much daylight was left when they kicked off. At Camus Place Primary school, he would make wicker baskets of dubious quality to sell around the doors of the neighbourhood with his classmates in order to buy strips for their first properly organised team and, once he had moved to Kingsridge Secondary School, a milk round would finance the purchase of a decent pair of football boots.

The undeniable promise that was sufficient to eventually carry him into the Scotland schoolboy side at Under 16 level seemed destined to go unnoticed by any senior club, however, as he played his last international match against England at Ibrox before going to college to study mechanical engineering. The only scout to have shown any interest up until then had been from Rangers, the team he had watched as a boy in the company of his father.

'The scout had seen me play for Queens Park Strollers and asked for my name. When he was told it was Danny McGrain there was no further interest shown. My interpretation of that was then, as it is now, that I was taken, mistakenly, to be Catholic by birth and rejected when, in fact, my full name of

Daniel Fergus McGrain had been handed down from generation to generation by my non-Catholic forebears on the Isle of
Skye.'

Rangers' loss would turn into Celtic's gain because, sitting
in the stand at Ibrox watching the schoolboys play was Tommy
Reilly, a friend of the then assistant manager at Celtic Park,
Sean Fallon. Because of its frequently dramatic content, it
must be one of the best-documented stories of modern times
that Danny, having served his time not in a technical college
but at the seat of advanced learning presided over by Jock
Stein, established himself in the Celtic first team only to be
struck down by a serious head injury while playing against
Falkirk at Brockville in 1972. Removal to a neuro-surgical hospital was thought of at one stage and there followed weeks of
double vision even after the idea had been discarded because
of the success of his recovery. Ultimately, though, Danny took
driving lessons and passed his test at the first time of asking to
prove to himself, and others, that his faculties were unim-
paired. The endurance that was to become synonymous with
his name also brought him back as strong as ever to Celtic
Park and led, within months of his accident, to his first representative honour, playing for Scotland's Under 23 side against
Wales.

His direct opponent was Leighton James, who was destined never to forget McGrain's name and be haunted by his
appearance in every match they played against each other
over the subsequent years. It is a matter of fact, and not conjec-
ture, that James rarely got a kick of the ball against Danny, who
was given an early indication that he had the psychological
advantage over his man.

'In one of the earliest full internationals we had against
Wales, Leighton came over to me just before the kick off and
said he hoped I had a good game. I knew then I had him in my
pocket. In the league I came from, the only time players spoke
to each other was to trade uncomplimentary remarks.'

Those were the days of barely diluted accomplishment for
Celtic on the domestic front, even if they were punctuated by
mishap for Danny. He was diagnosed as being diabetic on the

McGrain in the days when a close shave meant more than a narrow result.

day after Scotland's return from the World Cup finals of 1974 in West Germany but recovered from the shock by spending the remainder of the summer learning how to inject himself with insulin by practising on an orange and going on long road runs by himself to prove that his body could cope with this malfunction. At all times there was the ability to see the funny side of his situation, which is the most fundamental aspect of his character.

'I can remember taking my seat in the stand at Hampden before a Scotland match and being picked out by a spectator who was obviously not a Celtic supporter. 'McGrain, ya Fenian

B------!' he shouted up to me before realising the description was inaccurate and changed his insult to 'McGrain, ya diabetic B------!'

If name calling is never likely to hurt the seasoned professional, the bruises that would show were only around the corner for Danny, though. Celtic's ascendancy in Scotland had been uninterrupted for nine years, but with the retirement of Billy McNeill as club captain in 1975 and the health problems that afflicted Jock Stein from then on as well, the team seemed to become stricken by misfortune.

In October, 1977, following the transfer of Kenny Dalglish to Liverpool and the serious injuries that forced an end to the careers of Pat Stanton and Alfie Conn, Danny McGrain collided with one of his best friends in the game, John Blackley of Hibs, in a league match at Celtic Park, and was not seen again in a hooped jersey for fifteen months.

'At the highest level of club football, there is an attitude of mind shared by players that nothing as serious as that will ever befall them. In spite of being a diabetic who had once sustained a fractured skull, I was no different from the rest. The months of going around specialists in hospitals in Scotland and England before ultimately turning to acupuncture as a means of bringing about a cure had a profound effect on me, though. When I came back to play for Celtic it is true to say I was never the same player I had been, but the other side of the coin was that I appreciated the game for the game's sake all the more. In fact, I made myself feel that way. Every time I felt the old, complacent ways coming on again, I gave myself a stern talking to. It was too good a feeling just to put on a pair of boots again to take anything for granted beyond the next game I was about to play.'

The perception of those who did not support Celtic was that McGrain had turned into a more aggressive defender, trying to compensate for the lack of his old quickness of thought and deed by physical means.

'The crispness of my tackling was certainly never returned to me and the idea of overlapping as I had once done was out of the question as well, but I would maintain to this day that I was never a deliberately dirty player.'

The official seal was put on McGrain's rehabilitation, in fact, by Jock Stein in 1979 when, as Scotland manager, he chose him for the international against Belgium.

'I had come off Celtic's training ground at Barrowfield one wet and miserable Monday morning to be told by someone that I was in the Scotland squad but, to be honest, I didn't believe it. When I went back to Celtic Park, I asked Billy McNeill to confirm my selection with the S.F.A. The fact that I went on to gain another eighteen caps after that proved beyond doubt to me that big Jock was not acting out of sentimentality.'

McGrain's personal renaissance as Celtic's captain and a Scottish internationalist coincided with the club's restored status under Billy McNeill. The league title had been won twice and the Scottish Cup once before McGrain would be confronted by the player who, he would freely admit, got the better of him in front of his own crowd at Celtic Park, a rare distinction.

'If I had to pick one game I would not care to re-live it would be the one against Ajax in the European Cup at the start of the 1982-83 season. Celtic finally drew 2-2 on the night but I was given a roasting by Jesper Olsen on the wing. After I had played for so many years at a certain level in either the old First Division or the Premier League, Olsen suddenly introduced me to another dimension with his speed and trickery. In the expression of the fight game, I couldn't lay a glove on him. That had nothing at all to do with me being over thirty years old and with a long medical history behind me coming up against a much younger man. Even at my so-called peak I don't believe I could have done anything against him that night. The funny thing is, I have never seen Jesper play like that since then. In all the times I have watched him play since he left Holland to join Manchester United, he has never struck me as being as effective.'

Celtic supporters will have no difficulty recalling that, against all expectation, the Dutchmen could not capitalise on the advantage of having scored two goals in Glasgow and lost the return leg in Amsterdam, a tie in which Olsen was an infinitely more subdued player.

'It is the way of the professional game that I had to assert myself in that match by giving Jesper what we refer to in my business as a couple of whacks early on to see if it would act as a form of discouragement. There is no need for me to apologise for that. This is what goes on and there are very few professional players who do not accept that. Davie Cooper of Rangers, for instance, was extremely good at feinting past the full back and then making telling crosses with that good left foot of his. In all the matches we had against each other in the tense atmosphere of an Old Firm setting, I never once heard him complain to a referee about my tackling. Arthur Graham, when he played for Aberdeen before going to Leeds United, was another one who would keep coming back for more. He was exceptionally brave for a player of his slight build and he could use the ball a bit, too. That one night against Olsen, though, was probably my least enjoyable experience out of two decades in the game. Not even coming up against Jairzinho of Brazil for Scotland in the World Cup in 1974 can compare.'

In twenty years of accepting that there is no quarter given, and none asked, McGrain was sent off only once and the recollection is still irksome to him, even though it happened in 1982. The red card was shown by Andrew Waddell at Celtic Park in a league match against Aberdeen and for two separate offences against their winger, Peter Weir, although Danny would contest that the punishment fitted the crime. As there are players who roll with the flow, there are others, he believes, who supplement their natural abililty with a flair for showing their opponents in an unfavourable light,

'Peter Weir could be like that and on the fateful day he had me in the referee's book early on when I felt there was no justification because of his theatrics after I had tackled him. When I did commit a foul that was worthy of a caution, Mr Waddell then sent me off. It still annoys me because I wanted to go through all of my career without that kind of blemish against my name.'

If Danny McGrain's career, warts and all, might easily have lent itself to a screenplay, the author might have scripted the action to end and the credits to roll after what was a suitably climactic finish to the 1985-86 League Championship at Love

Celtic's most capped player in spite of a skull fracture, diabetes and the minor intrusion of a broken leg.

Street. Having led Celtic to victory in the historic one hundredth Scottish Cup final twelve months before, the captaincy on the day the title was won by virtue of a five-goal win over St. Mirren was a particularly pleasurable experience. Celtic's play in the first forty-five minutes of that match was irresistible, and for a veteran player who believed his best days were behind him McGrain rekindled the memory of how things had been with his involvement in the team's third goal.

'When I look at it again on film the move starts with me on the edge of Celtic's penalty area and finishes up with me standing inside St. Mirren's box. At the time, it seemed like the easiest eighty yards I had ever run and was typical of how we had won the flag by adhering to the club's traditional insistence on attack. There had been times when the lack of attention paid to the art of defending at Celtic Park was a frustrating experience, such as the game against Nottingham Forest there when we had played it from the heart instead of the head in the U.E.F.A. Cup and lost on aggregate after doing the hard part and getting a goalless draw in England. Sticking to the club's principles could have its moments, though, and Love Street that day was definitely one of them.'

The storyline did not end there, though, but took on a melancholy air instead after Paisley. A proposed move to leave Celtic and become the player-manager of Airdrie was derailed when his interview at Broomfield led to the directors turning him down as an applicant on a show of hands. Opinion had swung against him when, after he had offered a candid assessment of the club's youth recruitment policy, an air of concern arose over who might have to pay for hold-alls in the event of a nursery team being started. Those who had proposed McGrain had been so sure he was a candidate without rival that a celebration party had been arranged in licensed premises near to the ground, where the atmosphere was as chilled as the champagne once news of his rejection had been received.

Returning to Celtic Park, where, he would stress, there was never any hint of the club rubbing it in that they had done him a favour by offering him a new contract, McGrain was made club captain for what would turn out to be his last season while Roy Aitken assumed the leader's role on the park. Ironically for a man who never sought to draw attention to himself in the media throughout even the headiest days of his playing career — there are those among his peers who would say McGrain was totally withdrawn from his colleagues for many years until his long time out of the game brought about a mellowing of his personality — Danny became engulfed by publicity at the time when he parted company with Celtic. A time for sober reflection and a dignified withdrawal from the limelight turned giddy with allegations and recriminations.

An offer to become assistant manager at Celtic Park, extended to him by David Hay, was never permitted to be taken up and without, in McGrain's eyes, a satisfactory explanation ever being forthcoming. When, after a barren year for trophies, the time finally did come for Danny to go there was a sense of regret over how his free transfer was handled. McGrain would

Danny Boy — a Celtic Great in sunshine or in shadow.

maintain that his release was mismanaged and left him feeling embarrassed and hurt. On the day of what would turn out to be his last-ever appearance as a Celtic player at Celtic Park, there was still no official indication that he was going from the club. Celtic were playing Falkirk in the penultimate league game of the season and Danny would have welcomed the opportunity to take a symbolic leave of the supporters with whom he had enjoyed a special affinity beforehand.

The following Saturday, the final day of the season, the crossing of wires had reached the stage of tragi-comedy. In spite of witnessing their team lose to Hearts at Tynecastle on the afternoon Rangers were installed as Scottish League Champions for the first time in nine years, the Celtic support had stayed stoically cheering inside the ground, asking for a farewell appearance by the players.

Never having been one to see merit in taking a bow on the occasion of a defeat, Danny stayed in the dressing room, believing there would be another day for him to respond to such an invitation. But there never was. On the day he took his leave of Celtic, McGrain walked away from the ground as quietly as he had arrived on the Sunday afternoon, twenty years before, when he had signed his first contract. The disappointment was such he never returned to pick up his boots or the passport that was kept there for European travel with the team, arranging for them to be sent out to him. A meeting was fixed between Danny and the Celtic chairman, Jack McGinn, at which it was explained to him that, while the directors had known he was to be given a free transfer, they were not told exactly which day he was to sever his ties with the club.

The Celtic Supporters Association did make a formal presentation to him in recognition of all he had done for the team. The inscription on a mounted golden boot read: 'Presented to Danny McGrain by the affiliation of registered supporters clubs in appreciation of an outstanding career.' Offers to coach St. Johnstone and manage a team in Cyprus were then forthcoming but Danny went to Hamilton Accies instead to play for a side going for promotion to the Premier League and to take charge of their reserve team.

'I have to feel grateful to John Lambie for giving me the chance at Douglas Park to learn that side of the game without any pressures on me. It's not a case of the player who once competed at the highest level being unable to leave the game behind. I want to be involved in coaching because after all I learned at Celtic Park under Jock Stein and Billy McNeill, and the further education I received as part of the Scotland squad with men like Alex Ferguson and Jim McLean, it would have been a source of eternal regret for me not to have been given the opportunity to pass on what I had been given. Promotion for Hamilton to the Premier League has given me great personal satisfaction.'

The future for Danny McGrain will involve pursuing a career in that line, the past will cause him to be judged kindly in Celtic's history, no matter what.

## FULL INTERNATIONAL CAPS

### 1973

| | | | |
|---|---|---|---|
| May | Wales | (a) | 2-0 |
| May | N. Ireland | (h) | 1-2 |
| May | England | (a) | 0-1 |
| June | Switzerland | (a) | 0-1 |
| June | Brazil | (h) | 0-1 |
| Sept. | Czechoslovakia | (h) | 2-1 |
| Oct. | Czechoslovakia | (a) | 0-1 |
| Nov. | W. Germany | (h) | 1-1 |

### 1974

| | | | |
|---|---|---|---|
| May | Wales | (h) | 2-0 |
| May | England | (h) | 2-0 |
| June | Belgium | (a) | 1-2 |
| June | Norway | (a) | 2-1 |
| June | Zaire | (a) | 2-0 |
| June | Brazil | (a) | 0-0 |
| June | Yugoslavia | (a) | 1-1 |

### 1975

| | | | |
|---|---|---|---|
| Feb. | Spain | (a) | 1-1 |
| April | Sweden | (a) | 1-1 |
| May | Portugal | (h) | 1-0 |
| May | Wales | (a) | 2-2 |
| May | N. Ireland | (h) | 3-0 |
| May | England | (a) | 1-5 |
| June | Rumania | (a) | 1-1 |
| Sept. | Denmark | (a) | 1-0 |
| Oct. | Denmark | (h) | 3-1 |

### 1976

| | | | |
|---|---|---|---|
| April | Switzerland | (h) | 1-0 |
| May | Wales | (h) | 3-1 |
| May | N. Ireland | (h) | 3-0 |
| May | England | (h) | 2-1 |
| Sept. | Finland | (h) | 6-0 |
| Oct. | Czechoslovakia | (a) | 2-0 |
| Nov. | Wales | (h) | 1-0 |

### 1977

| | | | |
|---|---|---|---|
| April | Sweden | (h) | 3-1 |
| May | Wales | (a) | 0-0 |
| June | N. Ireland | (h) | 3-0 |
| June | England | (a) | 2-1 |

| June | Chile | (a) | 4·2 |
|------|-------|-----|-----|
| June | Argentina | (a) | 1·1 |
| June | Brazil | (a) | 2·0 |
| Sept. | E. Germany | (a) | 0·1 |
| Sept. | Czechoslovakia | (h) | 3·1 |

1979

| Dec. | Belgium | (h) | 3·1 |
|------|---------|-----|-----|

1980

| March | Portugal | (h) | 4·1 |
|-------|----------|-----|-----|
| May | N. Ireland | (a) | 0·1 |
| May | Wales | (h) | 1·0 |
| May | England | (h) | 0·2 |
| May | Poland | (a) | 0·1 |
| May | Hungary | (a) | 1·3 |
| Sept. | Sweden | (a) | 1·0 |
| Oct. | Portugal | (h) | 0·0 |

1981

| Feb. | Israel | (a) | 1·0 |
|------|--------|-----|-----|
| April | Israel | (h) | 3·1 |
| May | Wales | (a) | 0·2 |
| May | N. Ireland | (h) | 2·0 |
| May | England | (a) | 1·0 |
| Sept. | Sweden | (h) | 2·0 |

1982

| Feb. | Spain | (a) | 0·3 |
|------|-------|-----|-----|
| March | Holland | (h) | 2·1 |
| April | N. Ireland | (a) | 1·1 |
| May | England | (h) | 0·1 |
| June | N. Zealand | (a) | 5·2 |
| June | U.S.S.R. | (a) | 2·2 |

## CHAPTER NINE

# *Roy Aitken*

Roy Aitken is one of those players who can inspire extreme reactions in the people who watch him. The Celtic supporters adore the ground he walks upon, while the followers of the clubs he plays against tend simply to wish the earth would open and swallow him up. What would have to be commonly accepted, however, is that nobody deserves the honour of captaining Celtic in their centenary year more than him. By the end of the 1987-88 season, Roy Aitken had taken part in 600 competitive matches for the club, and by the time his present contract at Celtic Park expires in 1992, when he will be only 33

Roy Aitken: the Centenary Year captain. Nobody deserved the honour more.

years old, the likelihood is that the record books will need to be re-written to accommodate the fact that Robert Sime Aitken, to give him his proper name, has played more times for Celtic than anyone in its history. This accolade in the making, taken in conjunction with his captaincy of Scotland's national team, is all the more remarkable when it is considered that, up until he was twelve years of age, Roy had never taken part in an organised game of football. He was born the only child of John and Lily Aitken in the Ayrshire town of Ardrossan, where the local primary school he attended was so small there was no football team.

'I can remember my father buying me a leather ball when I was ten years old and walking down to the public park near our house with it tucked proudly underneath my arm. My dad had played the game for a side affiliated to the church we attended, St. Peter's Star of the Sea in Ardrossan. In fact, he had been a team-mate of the very young Bobby Lennox at one stage, something I was able to claim myself before I was much older, only this time as a professional with Celtic. Being an only child, and because both my parents worked, I think I had an inbred sense of responsibility. I have certainly never been unduly troubled by having to take things on my shoulders in the game.'

Roy's biographical details would lend weight to that theory. He was an established member of the Celtic first team before he left St. Andrew's Secondary school in Saltcoats, educated at both domestic and European level ahead of the formal examination results which brought him seven 'O' levels and four Higher certificates. He had also captained Celtic for the first time at the age of twenty and was the owner of League Championship and Scottish Cup winners medals before accepting the metaphorical key of the door. In the bad times, Roy's reluctance to accept defeat for Celtic earned him the respect of his fellow professionals along with the punishments that were handed out to him on a regular, and occasionally dramatic, basis by referees.

In spite of the fact that Aitken was ordered off in the Scottish Cup final of 1984 against Alex Ferguson's Aberdeen, the first player to suffer that particular indignity in fifty-five years since

Aitken salutes the fans who worship the ground he walks upon.

Jock Buchanan of Rangers, the then Pittodrie manager was fond of referring to him in private as 'John Wayne' for the qualities of leadership and endurance Roy would bring to his team whenever they were confronted with what was a seemingly lost cause. Alan Rough, who played against him as goalkeeper for Partick Thistle and Hibs as well as with him for Scotland, would endorse those sentiments by saying, 'You can almost hear a bugle blowing in the distance when Roy starts one of those runs of his from defence into attack.'

The highest form of tribute that was paid to him, though, came from Jock Stein during his time as manager of Celtic. After a year out of the game suffering from the effects of a car crash, during which time Aitken had made his debut and

retained his place at Celtic Park, Stein returned to the club convinced that too much had already been asked of a teenager
who was only learning the game in his absence.

'He took me to his office and explained to me that, in his
opinion, I did not have the physical strength as yet to play at the
centre of the defence, but stressed that he did not want me to
drop out of the side, either. The answer was to create a position
for me, which was what Mr Stein did, having the foresight to
use me directly in front of the back four where my youthful
exuberance could be put to more telling use. It was an idea that
Scotland would copy many years later to finally give me a role
to which I could adapt in the national side.'

Aitken's prodigious stamina, unaffected by twelve years of
playing at the highest level, had come to light after he had
begun to excel in a variety of sports at school. He became the
sports champion at St. Andrew's, in fact, for track and field
events and has since been told by Celtic's physiotherapist,
Brian Scott, that his strength is based on having been fortun-
ately blessed with strong knees and ankles which have
ensured that Roy can recall missing only one match in his
career with club or country because of injury.

Ayr United could have had first claim on the teenage pro-
tégé who was naturally proficient in everything he did, from
being chosen to represent Scotland at basketball to gaining a
diploma for playing the piano. When it came down to making
the choice between Somerset Park and Celtic Park, though,
the independent streak Roy had been born with enabled the
fourteen-year-old to make up his own mind without parental or
any other external influences. This caused him to come down
instinctively on the side of the bigger club.

'Naturally, I was warned that Celtic took on large numbers of
schoolboys every year, and that the odds against me ever making the breakthrough were considerable, whereas with Ayr
United I would have had a chance of coming to the fore more
easily. My attitude, however, was to take the best if it was offered
to you and aim for the top rather than start small and hope to
aspire to the big time one day.'

So it was, then, that the confirmed Celtic supporter, who

had never seen the team play nor even set his eyes on Celtic Park, came to find himself walking with his father from Glasgow's Central Station to the ground in order to put his name to a registration form. It has been said of Roy Aitken that, because of the circumstances which prevailed then, he had to be basically self-taught in the Premier League and everywhere else. Celtic, in the wake of Jock Stein's health problems and the transfer and injury difficulties which beset the club, were a team who had lost their way. This meant that the atmosphere was too unsettled for any of the more experienced players to nurse along the recruit from schools football, no matter how willing he might have been. It was a case of every man for himself, but the memory has left no mark on him.

'I watched good professionals beside me like Danny McGrain, Kenny Dalglish and Andy Lynch and if I had to pick up things as I went along, then I don't feel it has done me any harm in the long run.'

Along the way, though, Roy acquired the nickname of the 'Bear' that was taken by some to mean a player of unbridled aggression. Being sent off three times while playing for the Celtic managers he has worked under, Jock Stein, Billy McNeill and David Hay, did nothing to dissuade his detractors from that point of view. The player, naturally, does not accept that as being the case and feels that it is only now that he has been named as Scotland's squad captain by Andy Roxburgh, meaning that he is the international side's figurehead on and off the field, he has come to be seen in a more favourable light.

'I don't think I play the game any differently now from the way I did as a teenager when I first came into the Celtic team but international acceptance does tend to earn you an even break in the eyes of supporters, regardless of which team they follow. My interpretation of being called the 'Bear' is that it signifies a whole-hearted approach.'

His first dismissal, though, came in a Scottish Cup tie against Kilmarnock in 1977, when Celtic were eliminated by a side from a lower division for the first time in twenty-nine years. The club finished fifth in the league that same season, with as many losses as they had wins, and failed to qualify for a place in

Europe. His competitively combative instincts were used more productively when Billy McNeill assumed control of the team and Roy Aitken played a highly significant role in two memorable matches against Rangers within twelve months of each other that were to establish him as an essential part of the side.

In May, 1979, Celtic had to defeat their historic rivals at Celtic Park by way of completing what would be a breathtaking run from an apparently indifferent position in mid-table to accepting the title of League champions. A goal down and reduced to only ten men following the ordering off of the late Johnny Doyle, Celtic were brought back into the game by Aitken's equalising goal and also by the sight of him covering every inch of the playing surface like a one-man swarm. When George McCluskey put Celtic in front, the ground filled with 52,000 people took on the atmosphere of the madhouse, only to have the home support rendered lifeless by a goal from Robert Russell that restored equality. There were only eight minutes remaining for play and heroic failure, creditable but worthless, looked to be at hand. An own goal from Rangers' Colin Jackson, however, was like the belated bursting of a dam and by time-up Celtic had flooded past the Rangers defence yet again, contriving to make it seem as if the numerical burden was not theirs but belonged to the visiting side instead. Murdo Macleod's last-minute goal brought to a close a match that would be vivid in the memory long after the whistle had blown.

A year later at Hampden Park, Celtic were similarly disadvantaged when, in the lead-up to the Scottish Cup final against Rangers, the club lost the services of their two centre backs, Roddie McDonald and Tom McAdam, because of suspension. Aitken was called up to discipline himself to a defensive role beside the adaptable Michael Conroy.

'Being written off before the event, as we were, always acts as an added incentive to players, especially Celtic players, and I think we proved that by eventually winning by the only goal of the game on that occasion.'

The graph of any player's career always takes on the shape of a mountain range, being full of peaks and valleys, and the

Aitken: competitive, combative, Alex Ferguson called him 'John Wayne.'

highlights contained within Roy Aitken's domestic commit-
ments at that time were only in marked contrast to the disappointment he suffered by dropping out of the international
scene to the extent that, over the next five years, he played only
eleven times for his country.

'I was always one of those who felt a deep sense of privilege
whenever I was asked to turn out for Scotland, and that was
why I willingly agreed to act so often as the over-age player in
the Under 21 side during that fallow period. There does come a
time, however, when you have to stop and ask yourself if too
many appearances at that level can become counter produc-
tive. It is, after all, supposed to be a job for a vastly experienced
player who is able to lend a hand to the younger ones around
about him. That was how I came to approach Walter Smith,
who is now Rangers' assistant manager but was then with

Dundee United as well as helping out Jock Stein with the international players, and asked him if this was all they had in mind
for me. Walter reassured me that the big man had taken notice
of everything I had done, and in 1983 I once again claimed a
more settled place with the full international side, mainly due, I
always thought, to the influence that Alex Ferguson was by
then exerting over Mr Stein.'

That return would coincide, though, with an internal rift at
Celtic Park that saw Billy McNeill depart the manager's office
after winning the club three championships, the League Cup
and the Scottish Cup. Roy Aitken and Celtic simultaneously
embarked on a turbulent phase.

David Hay had gone from Celtic to join Chelsea the year
before Roy came to the club. His return as manager was under
the most trying circumstances imaginable, the acrimony sur-
rounding McNeill's waygoing leading into a time when high
drama and low farce visited Celtic by turns, proving that the
unusual never comes at any extra cost where this club is
concerned.

The lowest point on a personal level for Roy Aitken came
when he was sent off by the referee, Bob Valentine, for a tackle
on Mark McGhee, then of Aberdeen, in the Scottish Cup final.
To this day the Celtic captain still protests his innocence over
the challenge that led to him being dismissed in the first half of
a game that had already seen Aberdeen take the lead. The
basis of his defence is that while his tackle had its roots in tactical destruction, it was not a case of premeditated violence.

'I caught Mark with my hand in an awkward way rather than
anything else, but the referee was in no doubt I had to go and I
was angry at the time that he might have been helped in reaching that decision by the Aberdeen players who crowded round
Mr. Valentine offering their version of events.'

There was a heavy irony still to come, too, in that McGhee
would eventually score the winning goal in extra time and then
receive the sponsor's prize for being voted the fittest player on
the park by a panel of watching journalists, each distinction
calling the ferocity of the Celtic player's collision with him into
deeper doubt. A silent onlooker from the directors' box as the

remainder of the game unfolded after his withdrawal, Aitken refused to take part in the ceremony of handing out the medals to the winners and losers and asked his friend and team-mate, Mark Reid, to collect it on his behalf. In the embittered atmosphere of the Celtic dressing room afterwards David Hay took his player to one side and said the club would either have to 'change your position or your club.' If the former might have been acceptable, the latter most certainly was not.

'No matter what happened, I was determined that nothing would drive me away from Scotland or from Celtic. They were the only team I had ever wanted to play for and I had even prided myself on proving that by always signing a new contract before the terms of the old one had expired. I was also certain in my own mind that I had done nothing at Hampden that day to make the club feel ashamed of me.'

As if to underline the depth of his own conviction, Aitken did as he had promised to do later that same day and attended a Celtic supporters' club function in Coatbridge, seeing no need to go into hiding. The attitude of the fans is a fickle and unpredictable thing, however, and Roy Aitken had to endure a time as an outcast from their affections when, in relatively quick succession, they found him guilty of complicity as Celtic went out of the U.E.F.A. Cup to Nottingham Forest at home after getting a promising, goalless draw in the Midlands, and then lost in the final of the Skol Cup to Rangers. This upset came after the period of extra time that was turning into an agonising ritual for Celtic players and followers alike, initially promising belated hope of a win but actually turning out to be only a means of prolonging the agony. In that match Aitken gave away the penalty kick that won the trophy for Rangers as Ally McCoist, the player he impeded, scored after Pat Bonner had parried his original effort. Retribution is always swift after a disappointment on that scale and Aitken was only too conscious of the chill from the fans' antagonism on his back.

'I think all players who have been with one club for a long time experience these feelings of rejection at one stage. If you analyse it, very few people nowadays stay with one club for very long and for those who do familiarity can sometimes breed contempt.'

The game itself has ways of compensating for the blows it inflicts on the unsuspecting, though, and Aitken was to be repaid in full during the Scottish Cup final of 1985 and the League Championship campaign that came the season immediately after.

David Hay, for all that he was maligned by some Celtic fans, provided them with two genuinely unforgettable days, moments that would compare easily with any fabled extract from Celtic's back pages. On the 18th of May, 1985, in what was the historic one hundredth Scottish Cup final, Celtic trailed Dundee United by a Stuart Beedie goal with fifteen minutes to go of a match in which they had gradually run out of ideas and inspiration. The free kick from which Davie Provan equalised, however, was the stuff of divine intervention and, with six minutes left, it was from a cross by a now highly moti-vated Roy Aitken that Frank McGarvey headed the winner in front of a Celtic end that had been trying to suck the ball to-wards Hamish McAlpine's goal for the whole of the second half. If the crowd scenes that day could have been construed as a celebration of the will of the people proving itself to work, they were matched only by those on the final day of the following season when Celtic took the league title from Hearts' grasp by virtue of winning by five clear goals at Love Street against St. Mirren while the Edinburgh club lost their match away from home to Dundee with two goals scored in the last seven minutes by Albert Kidd.

Celtic supporters at Paisley, apparently blessed for the day with powers of bi-location, seemed to know the score one hun-dred miles away even before it had been officially relayed to them by assorted newspaper, radio and television men, and the Celtic players responded to the two separate eruptions on the terracing as the final whistle neared.

In this moment of uncertainty over the future of Danny McGrain, Celtic's triumph also marked David Hay's decision to split the captaincy of the club into two defined roles. McGrain would be known thereafter as club captain, while Roy Aitken assumed the duties of leader on the field. The promotion from the ranks coincided with his testimonial year but that would

Roy as Scotland's captain, pointing the way to the next World Cup?

lead, ironically, to Celtic getting their only trophy of a careworn season as they defeated Manchester United for a cup without kudos.

Roy Aitken is particularly conscious of the fact that he does not want to lead the Celtic team throughout a period of domination by the club's greatest rivals, Rangers.

'John Greig was a man I had a lot of time for when he was the captain at Ibrox, but I have an idea how he must have felt when that honour came at a time when Celtic were the pre-eminent club in Scotland on the continent. I would not like to live through something similar.'

The reinstatement of Billy McNeill as manager in May, 1987 instantly convinced those with Celtic at heart that this would not be the case and Aitken was among the first converts.

'On his first day back, he called all the players to the ground and spoke to us in that inspirational way of his about how

Rangers, with Graeme Souness and an unlimited supply of money, had thrown down the gauntlet to Celtic. Billy used his right hand, extended at head height, to denote Rangers' status and put his left hand further down to let us know where Celtic stood. It was made plain that Billy expected the scales to be tipped the other way eventually. He is such a fanatical Celtic man, the only one who could have managed the club in its centenary year, that you felt you would only let him down at your peril.'

## FULL INTERNATIONAL CAPS

| | | | |
|---|---|---|---|
| **1979** | | | |
| Sept. | Peru | (h) | 1-1 |
| Dec. | Belgium | (h) | 1-3 |
| **1980** | | | |
| May | Wales | (h) | 1-0 |
| May | England | (h) | 0-2 |
| May | Poland | (a) | 0-1 |
| **1982** | | | |
| Dec. | Belgium | (a) | 2-3 |
| **1983** | | | |
| June | Canada | (a) | 3-0 |
| June | Canada | (a) | 2-0 |
| Oct. | Belgium | (h) | 1-1 |
| Dec. | N. Ireland | (a) | 0-2 |
| **1984** | | | |
| Feb. | Wales | (h) | 2-1 |
| May | England | (h) | 1-0 |
| May | Iceland | (a) | 1-0 |
| **1985** | | | |
| May | England | (h) | 1-0 |
| Sept. | Wales | (a) | 1-1 |
| Oct. | E. Germany | (h) | 0-0 |
| Nov. | Australia | (h) | 2-0 |
| Dec. | Australia | (a) | 0-0 |
| **1986** | | | |
| Jan. | Israel | (a) | 1-0 |

| March | Rumania | (h) | 3-0 |
|-------|---------|-----|-----|
| April | England | (a) | 1-2 |
| June | Denmark | (a) | 0-1 |
| June | W. Germany | (a) | 1-2 |
| June | Uruguay | (a) | 0-0 |
| Sept. | Bulgaria | (h) | 0-0 |
| Oct. | Eire | (a) | 0-0 |
| Nov. | Luxembourg | (h) | 3-0 |

**1987**

| Feb. | Eire | (h) | 0-1 |
|------|------|-----|-----|
| April | Belgium | (a) | 1-4 |
| May | England | (h) | 0-0 |
| May | Brazil | (h) | 0-2 |
| Sept. | Hungary | (h) | 3-0 |
| Nov. | Bulgaria | (a) | 1-0 |
| Nov. | Belgium | (h) | 2-0 |
| Dec. | Luxembourg | (a) | 0-0 |

**1988**

| Feb. | Saudi Arabia | (a) | 2-2 |
|------|--------------|-----|-----|
| March | Malta | (a) | 1-1 |
| April | Spain | (a) | 0-0 |
| May | Colombia | (a) | 0-0 |
| May | England | (a) | 0-1 |

# CHAPTER TEN

## *Paul McStay*

The day after Celtic beat Dundee United and won the Scottish Cup for a record 28th time, and in a manner that was entirely typical of the course of the season that was partly contained within their centenary year, Paul McStay was awarded the accolade of Player of the Year by his fellow professionals in the Scottish Professional Footballers Association. In the course of his acceptance speech, during which he remarked that it had been a 'joy' to play alongside men of the calibre of those who had come back from a goal down to win the cup with two of

Paul McStay receives his award as the Scottish Professional Footballers' Association's Player of the Year, 1988.

their own in the last fifteen minutes of the match, Paul touched on the identity of the person who had, he felt, guided him to the distinction of being undeniably the best player in the country, Billy McNeill. For at least two of the four years McNeill had spent in involuntary exile away from Celtic Park, the previously breathtaking heights which McStay was capable of reaching no matter the opposition went unrecorded and his form slumped to such a degree that there were dark rumours of illness and suggestions that a precocious talent had burned itself out as quickly as it had first come to light. It would be possible to argue now, however, that the catalyst for Celtic's League and Cup-winning season was Paul McStay, and that the day he started in earnest to become so was Friday, December 4, 1987. It was then that Billy McNeill, the excitement easily recognisable in his voice, announced that his young player had signed a new, five-year contract with the club, thereby dispelling rumours of a possible move to the continent . . .

Billy McNeill and Paul McStay had first come into contact nine years earlier, brought together by a legally binding agreement of another kind. When Jock Stein ceased to be Celtic's manager, McNeill inherited, amongst other things, two youthful brothers on his playing staff, Willie and Paul McStay. Both had been brought to Celtic Park by Sean Fallon, the only difference being that while Willie was old enough to sign the form that registered him with the club, Paul was then still under the age of consent for such an undertaking. He was affiliated to Celtic only through the emotional bond that connected his family to the team for which his great uncles, Jimmy and Willie, had played and attained legendary status between the wars.

As he approached his thirteenth birthday, when he would, if he wished, be able to make legitimate his love affair with Celtic, Paul McStay was the best-known young player in Scotland and the object of attention for every club scout who had ambitions to make a name for himself by being the one to somehow get Paul to renounce his origins and sign for them. Unlike a contemporary of his, Kevin Gallacher of Dundee United, who was the grandson of the inimitable Patsy and whose outstanding talent was proof of his being heir to more than just the family name, Paul had no difficulty in reconciling himself to the ideal of constantly having the past paraded in front of him and vague comparisons being made. His father, John, was obsessive about the club and had brought up his sons to share that regard for Celtic. The fact that the family home was, and still is, in the Lanarkshire town of Larkhall, where, it is rumoured, Celtic supporters can only be found by using a geiger counter in an area densely populated by those whose allegiance is fanatically pledged to the other half of the Old Firm, made the conviction all the more strongly felt.

So it was, that Billy McNeill and his newly appointed chief scout, John Kelman, were able to approach the question of signing Paul McStay without any feeling of trepidation, even though English sides like Everton, Leeds and Spurs could have made offers of recompense for their son's signature that would have turned many an ordinary parent's head. Kelman is another steeped in Celtic's lore, who tends to perceive any criticism of the team as the ultimate heresy and those who succumb to the temptation to be morally misguided. As a purveyor of teenage talent that will eventually blossom at Celtic Park with only the ordinary amount of fine tuning, Kelman has to be occasionally brutally frank in his assessment of certain individuals. To hear him speak about Paul McStay is to be encouraged to look around for the sudden intrusion of a pianist who will set his words to music.

'Only a masochist could find a serious flaw in Paul McStay, either as a player or as a human being. Sometimes I wonder, in fact, if Paul might not have made an even better player if he had possessed a bigger ego, but I would never want to change him. For me — and I have said this to his face in front of company — Paul McStay is the best player I have ever seen at Celtic Park. I had a very healthy respect for people like Bobby Evans in the fifties and then Paddy Crerand in the decade after that but, for awareness and skill, Paul is better than any of them, including Kenny Dalglish. He is a world-renowned player, the only difference is he doesn't know it and certainly doesn't act like it off the field.'

'It has often struck me as being funny that, even during the

McStay — the best ever at Celtic Park?

winning of the League and Cup double, the huge crowds Celtic got nearly always reserved their chanting for other players besides Paul, even though he was having a season that was officially recognised by his colleagues, the sports writers and those who sponsor the game as being without equal among rival, or even fellow-Celtic players. But, then, he is not a night clubber or the type to draw any kind of attention to himself. Essentially, Paul is still a Celtic supporter who also has a contract to play for the club.'

The return of Billy McNeill to Celtic Park was the dream that little children were told by anxious parents to include in their bedtime prayers for the attention of the appropriate ear in case it could be turned into reality during the mid-eighties when the club, which showed signs of unsteadiness that threatened to turn into something even more pitiable, was staggering towards its one hundredth birthday. The homecoming, when it was made public, excited more than the terracing dwellers who revered McNeill's name. Paul McStay, for one, was approaching the end of his contract, and his tether, simultaneously at Celtic Park. He had made his debut for the first team at the age of 17 in a win over Aberdeen at Pittodrie six years earlier and would never know what it was to be a reserve-team player. Even as a schoolboy at Holy Cross in Hamilton and then as an amateur player with Hamilton Thistle, Paul was used to competing against boys two years older than himself and when, at the age of sixteen, he had graduated to Celtic Boys' Club, Billy McNeill could stand the wait no longer and called him up to immerse him in the ways of his team.

The Boys' Club were in the final of the Scottish Under 16's cup, too, but the manager, during his first stay with Celtic, removed McStay on the eve of the game to play for the reserves instead. The relationship between player and manager was mutually beneficial, something that was probably best highlighted by two things, the severe loss of confidence suffered by McStay while his mentor was away and the willingness of the player to commit himself to a long-term contract within months of McNeill's return.

'I got so excited about Celtic's future when the manager started to talk to me that I went outside his office with my father, had a quick conversation, and went back in offering to sign on for another ten years. For me, all the doubts over Celtic's level of ambition were removed when the board of directors went for the manager everybody wanted. Once he was in the job, I knew

When Paul plays, Celtic play!

I wanted my future with Celtic settled once and for all. It was the manager, though, who said it would be best for all concerned if I signed for five years, and whatever he says . . . . '

The irony of the situation is that, for all his devotion to Billy McNeill, the moments that Paul McStay will treasure above all with Celtic were all gathered while David Hay was in charge of the team. The examples Paul would give are a key to his personality and what was going through his mind when negotiating the contract that pleased the Celtic supporters so much an outsider might have thought he was giving them a share of his wages.

'The first was an Old Firm game at Celtic Park when Willie and myself became the first set of brothers since our great uncles to play for one half of the Old Firm against the other and finish on the winning side as well. Two years later, we not only played together against Rangers but each scored a goal in Celtic's win. The last, great memory was of the 1985 Scottish Cup final, when we defeated Dundee United so dramatically with two goals in the last quarter of an hour. To be on the park with your own brother at the end of an occasion like that is a feeling that is indescribable. The family are my bedrock, which is why I found it so distressing when Willie was transferred to England by Celtic. My younger brother, Raymond, is now a Celtic player, however, and it is my ambition to play in the first team beside him one day. The McStay name and the family's historical link with Celtic is something that has always made me feel proud and I'm certainly not intimidated when the older generation take me aside at supporters' functions and go on about their recollections of my great uncles and the games they saw them play. I feel happy about the fact they gave so many people such pleasure. I feel able to handle all aspects of my life in a more mature fashion now. If any player lets the spotlight get to him, he can have severe problems off the park but I have my parents, my brothers and now my wife, Anne-Marie, to support me away from the game.'

'So far as playing is concerned, I feel much stronger, too. I know there were stories that I had contracted an illness after returning from the 1986 World Cup in Mexico, and others that I

'My fitness can't be in doubt when I was part of a Celtic side that won so many matches in the final minutes.'

was really an asthmatic, which apparently explained an inability to last the full ninety minutes, but the fitness of all the players who took part in the winning of the double surely put any of those stories into perspective. We won so many matches late on because Celtic's strength was at an impressively high level. The truth is a number of factors combined to put me off form for a long while. Being a young starter in the team, I naturally found there came a time when the incessant pressure on the park that comes with being a Celtic player and a Scottish internationalist got the better of me. I was also still learning my job as a player, no matter how long I had been in the first team. As well as that, good friends like Charlie Nicholas and Frank McGarvey had moved on and I had to come to terms with all of that . . .'

There are, as John Kelman said, only those who would enjoy banging their head off a brick wall who would attempt to tell you now that Paul McStay has not recovered to the extent that he is the most influential player currently at Billy McNeill's disposal. If there is a flaw, and nobody mentioned infallibility in even this extraordinary case, it would be, on the player's own admission, a failure to score as often as he might. There were certain memorable examples during what will become enshrined as the centenary championship which suggested the fault is not irreparable, like the vicious drive that brought an apparently lost cause against Hearts back to life at Celtic Park, when a two-goal deficit was erased in the last ten minutes of play. The goal scored on the volley against Rangers at Ibrox two months later helped bring the championship flag more clearly into focus and was a startling reminder that even people with the looks, and the disposition, of a choirboy can get a little venomous when the mood is on them.

'When Paul McStay plays, Celtic play,' was a quote recited like a well-remembered piece of poetry by Billy McNeill throughout that season and offered by way of explanation for the gift to change, or dictate, the course of any game on the road to the double. A single pass that was struck through the heart of a bemused Rangers defence to Chris Morris for him to create a goal for Frank McAvennie in another Old Firm match aroused as much comment as the rest of the game.

McStay's place in a book devoted to Celtic's truly great players should not be questioned on the grounds of age or length of service. If the man paid to bring the club the best players — and nine of the double-winning squad were signed by John Kelman — can describe him as the best in his lifetime, and Billy McNeill is moved by the capture of his signature on a lengthy contract, it ought to be futile saying anything else. All that remains to be recorded is that when Paul McStay was approached for an interview by the author and told the purpose of our conversation he was genuinely touched by his inclusion among such company and gave self-conscious hints of a mistake having been made somewhere.

There is no error, of course, and Paul McStay, role model for the young supporters in the early years of the club's next century, is an obvious choice because he easily fulfils all the criteria for greatness within the context of Celtic football club and their remarkable and praiseworthy traditions.

## FULL INTERNATIONAL CAPS

**1983**

| | | | |
|---|---|---|---|
| Sept. | Uruguay | (h) | 2-0 |
| Oct. | Belgium | (h) | 1-1 |
| Nov. | E. Germany | (a) | 1-2 |
| Dec. | N. Ireland | (a) | 0-2 |

**1984**

| | | | |
|---|---|---|---|
| Feb. | Wales | (h) | 2-1 |
| May | England | (h) | 1-1 |
| Oct. | Iceland | (h) | 3-0 |
| Nov. | Spain | (h) | 3-1 |

**1985**

| | | | |
|---|---|---|---|
| Feb. | Spain | (a) | 0-1 |
| Mar. | Wales | (h) | 0-1 |
| Oct. | E. Germany | (h) | 0-0 |
| Dec. | Australia | (a) | 0-0 |

**1986**

| | | | |
|---|---|---|---|
| Jan. | Israel | (a) | 1-0 |
| June | Uruguay | (a) | 0-0 |
| Sept. | Bulgaria | (h) | 0-0 |
| Oct. | Eire | (a) | 0-0 |
| Nov. | Luxembourg | (h) | 3-0 |

**1987**

| | | | |
|---|---|---|---|
| Feb. | Eire | (h) | 0-1 |
| April | Belgium | (a) | 1-4 |
| May | England | (h) | 0-0 |
| May | Brazil | (h) | 0-2 |
| Sept. | Hungary | (h) | 3-0 |
| Oct. | Belgium | (h) | 2-0 |

| Nov. | Bulgaria | (a) | 1·0 |
| Dec. | Luxembourg | (a) | 1·0 |
| 1988 | | | |
| Feb. | Saudi Arabia | (a) | 2·2 |
| April | Spain | (a) | 0·0 |
| May | Colombia | (h) | 0·0 |
| May | England | (a) | 0·1 |

# Celtic Facts

## *Championship Points '47 to '88*

| YEAR | PLACE | GAMES | POINTS |
|------|-------|-------|--------|
| 1947 | 7th | 30 | 32 |
| 1948 | 12th | 30 | 25 |
| 1949 | 6th | 30 | 31 |
| 1950 | 5th | 30 | 35 |
| 1951 | 7th | 30 | 29 |
| 1952 | 9th | 30 | 28 |
| 1953 | 8th | 30 | 29 |
| 1954 | 1st | 30 | 43 |
| 1955 | 2nd | 30 | 46 |
| 1956 | 5th | 34 | 41 |
| 1957 | 5th | 34 | 38 |
| 1958 | 3rd | 34 | 46 |
| 1959 | 6th | 34 | 36 |
| 1960 | 9th | 34 | 33 |
| 1961 | 4th | 34 | 39 |
| 1962 | 3rd | 34 | 46 |
| 1963 | 4th | 34 | 44 |
| 1964 | 3rd | 34 | 47 |
| 1965 | 8th | 34 | 37 |
| 1966 | 1st | 34 | 57 |
| 1967 | 1st | 34 | 58 |
| 1968 | 1st | 34 | 63 |
| 1969 | 1st | 34 | 54 |
| 1970 | 1st | 34 | 57 |
| 1971 | 1st | 34 | 56 |
| 1972 | 1st | 34 | 60 |
| 1973 | 1st | 34 | 57 |
| 1974 | 1st | 34 | 53 |
| 1975 | 3rd | 34 | 45 |
| 1976 | 2nd | 36 | 48 |
| 1977 | 1st | 36 | 55 |
| 1978 | 5th | 36 | 36 |
| 1979 | 1st | 36 | 48 |
| 1980 | 2nd | 36 | 47 |
| 1981 | 1st | 36 | 56 |
| 1982 | 1st | 36 | 55 |
| 1983 | 2nd | 36 | 55 |
| 1984 | 2nd | 36 | 50 |
| 1985 | 2nd | 36 | 52 |
| 1986 | 1st | 36 | 50 |
| 1987 | 2nd | 44 | 63 |
| 1988 | 1st | 44 | 72 |

## SCOTTISH CUP RECORD

| | | | |
|---|---|---|---|
| 1946-47 | 1st rd | Dundee v Celtic | 2-1 |
| 1947-48 | 2nd rd | Celtic v Cowdenbeath | 3-0 |
| | 3rd rd | Celtic v Motherwell | 1-0 |
| | 4th rd | Celtic v Montrose | 4-0 |
| | Semi | Morton v Celtic | 1-0 |
| 1948-49 | 1st rd | Dundee United v Celtic | 4-3 |
| 1949-50 | 1st rd | Brechin City v Celtic | 0-3 |
| | 2nd rd | Third Lanark v Celtic | 1-1, 4-1 |
| | 3rd rd | Celtic v Aberdeen | 0-1 |
| 1950-51 | 1st rd | East Fife v Celtic | 2-2, 4-2 |
| | 2nd rd | Celtic v Duns | 4-0 |
| | 3rd rd | Hearts v Celtic | 1-2 |
| | 4th rd | Celtic v Aberdeen | 3-0 |
| | Semi | Celtic v Raith Rovers | 3-2 |
| | Final | Celtic v Motherwell | 1-0 |
| 1951-52 | 1st rd | Celtic v Third Lanark | 0-0, 1-2 |
| 1952-53 | 1st rd | Eyemouth v Celtic | 0-4 |
| | 2nd rd | Stirling Albion v Celtic | 1-1, 3-0 |
| | 3rd rd | Falkirk v Celtic | 2-3 |
| | 4th rd | Rangers v Celtic | 2-0 |
| 1953-54 | 2nd rd | Falkirk v Celtic | 1-2 |
| | 3rd rd | Stirling Albion v Celtic | 3-4 |
| | 4th rd | Hamilton Acas. v Celtic | 1-2 |
| | Semi | Celtic v Motherwell | 2-2, 3-1 |
| | Final | Aberdeen v Celtic | 1-2 |
| 1954-55 | 1st rd | Alloa v Celtic | 2-4 |
| | 2nd rd | Kilmarnock v Celtic | 1-1, 1-0 |
| | 3rd rd | Celtic v Hamilton Acas. | 2-1 |
| | Semi | Airdrie v Celtic | 2-2, 2-0 |
| | Final | Celtic v Clyde | 1-1, 0-1 |
| 1955-56 | 5th rd | Morton v Celtic | 0-2 |
| | 6th rd | Ayr v Celtic | 0-3 |
| | Q. Final | Celtic v Airdrie | 2-1 |
| | Semi | Celtic v Clyde | 2-1 |
| | Final | Hearts v Celtic | 3-1 |
| 1956-57 | 5th rd | Forres v Celtic | 0-5 |
| | 6th rd | Celtic v Rangers | 4-4, 0-2 |
| | Q. Final | Celtic v St. Mirren | 2-1 |
| | Semi | Celtic v Kilmarnock | 1-1, 3-1 |
| 1957-58 | 1st rd | Airdrie v Celtic | 3-4 |
| | 2nd rd | Celtic v Stirling Albion | 7-2 |
| | 3rd rd | Celtic v Clyde | 0-2 |
| 1958-59 | 1st rd | Celtic v Albion Rovers | 4-0 |
| | 2nd rd | Celtic v Clyde | 1-1, 3-4 |
| | 3rd rd | Celtic v Rangers | 2-1 |
| | 4th rd | Stirling Albion v Celtic | 1-3 |

| | | | |
|---|---|---|---|
| | Semi | St. Mirren v Celtic | 4-0 |
| 1959-60 | 2nd rd | St. Mirren v Celtic | 1-1, 4-4, 5-2 |
| | 3rd rd | Elgin City v Celtic | 1-2 |
| | 4th rd | Celtic v Partick Thistle | 2-0 |
| | Semi | Rangers v Celtic | 1-1, 1-4 |
| 1960-61 | 1st rd | Falkirk v Celtic | 1-3 |
| | 2nd rd | Celtic v Montrose | 6-0 |
| | 3rd rd | Raith Rovers v Celtic | 1-4 |
| | 4th rd | Celtic v Hibs | 1-1, 0-1 |
| | Semi | Celtic v Airdrie | 4-0 |
| | Final | Celtic v Dunfermline | 0-0, 2-0 |
| 1961-62 | 1st rd | Celtic v Cowdenbeath | 5-1 |
| | 2nd rd | Morton v Celtic | 1-3 |
| | 3rd rd | Hearts v Celtic | 3-4 |
| | Q. Final | Celtic v Third Lanark | 4-4, 4-0 |
| | Semi | Celtic v St. Mirren | 1-3 |
| 1962-63 | 1st rd | Falkirk v Celtic | 0-2 |
| | 2nd rd | Celtic v Hearts | 3-1 |
| | 3rd rd | Celtic v Gala Fairydean | 6-0 |
| | 4th rd | St. Mirren v Celtic | 0-1 |
| | Semi | Celtic v Raith Rovers | 5-2 |
| | Final | Rangers v Celtic | 3-0 |
| 1963-64 | 1st rd | Celtic v Eyemouth | 3-0 |
| | 2nd rd | Morton v Celtic | 1-3 |
| | 3rd rd | Celtic v Airdrie | 4-1 |
| | 4th rd | Rangers v Celtic | 2-0 |
| 1964-65 | 1st rd | St. Mirren v Celtic | 0-3 |
| | 2nd rd | Queens Park v Celtic | 0-1 |
| | 3rd rd | Celtic v Kilmarnock | 3-2 |
| | Semi | Motherwell v Celtic | 2-2, 3-0 |
| | Final | Celtic v Dunfermline | 3-2 |
| 1965-66 | 1st rd | Celtic v Stranraer | 4-0 |
| | 2nd rd | Dundee v Celtic | 0-2 |
| | 3rd rd | Hearts v Celtic | 3-3, 3-1 |
| | Semi | Celtic v Dunfermline | 2-0 |
| | Final | Rangers v Celtic | 0-0, 1-0 |
| 1966-67 | 1st rd | Celtic v Arbroath | 4-0 |
| | 2nd rd | Celtic v Elgin | 7-0 |
| | 3rd rd | Celtic v Queens Park | 5-3 |
| | Semi | Celtic v Clyde | 0-0, 2-0 |
| | Final | Celtic v Aberdeen | 2-0 |
| 1967-68 | 1st rd | Celtic v Dunfermline | 0-2 |
| 1968-69 | 1st rd | Partick Thistle v Celtic | 3-3, 8-1 |
| | 2nd rd | Clyde v Celtic | 0-0, 3-0 |
| | 3rd rd | Celtic v St. Johnstone | 3-2 |
| | Semi | Celtic v Morton | 4-1 |
| | Final | Celtic v Rangers | 4-0 |
| 1969-70 | 1st rd | Celtic v Dunfermline | 2-1 |

| | | | |
|---|---|---|---|
| | 2nd rd | Celtic v Dundee United | 4-0 |
| | 3rd rd | Celtic v Rangers | 3-1 |
| | Semi | Celtic v Dundee | 2-1 |
| | Final | Aberdeen v Celtic | 3-1 |
| 1970-71 | 3rd rd | Celtic v Q.O.S. | 5-1 |
| | 4th rd | Celtic v Dunfermline | 1-1, 1-0 |
| | 5th rd | Celtic v Raith Rovers | 7-1 |
| | Semi | Celtic v Airdrie | 3-3, 0-2 |
| | Final | Celtic v Rangers | 1-1, 1-2 |
| 1971-72 | 3rd rd | Celtic v Albion Rovers | 5-0 |
| | 4th rd | Celtic v Dundee | 4-0 |
| | 5th rd | Celtic v Hearts | 1-1, 1-0 |
| | Semi | Kilmarnock v Celtic | 1-3 |
| | Final | Celtic v Hibs | 6-1 |
| 1972-73 | 3rd rd | Celtic v East Fife | 4-1 |
| | 4th rd | Motherwell v Celtic | 0-4 |
| | 5th rd | Celtic v Aberdeen | 0-0, 0-1 |
| | Semi | Celtic v Dundee | 0-0, 0-3 |
| | Final | Celtic v Rangers | 2-3 |
| 1973-74 | 3rd rd | Celtic v Clydebank | 6-1 |
| | 4th rd | Celtic v Stirling Albion | 6-1 |
| | 5th rd | Celtic v Motherwell | 2-2, 0-1 |
| | Semi | Celtic v Dundee | 1-0 |
| | Final | Celtic v Dundee United | 3-0 |
| 1974-75 | 3rd rd | Hibs v Celtic | 0-2 |
| | 4th rd | Celtic v Clydebank | 4-1 |
| | 5th rd | Dumbarton v Celtic | 1-2 |
| | Semi | Celtic v Dundee | 1-0 |
| | Final | Celtic v Airdrie | 3-1 |
| 1975-76 | 3rd rd | Motherwell v Celtic | 3-2 |
| 1976-77 | 3rd rd | Airdrie v Celtic | 1-1, 5-0 |
| | 4th rd | Celtic v Ayr Utd | 1-1, 1-3 |
| | 5th rd | Celtic v Q.O.S. | 5-1 |
| | Semi | Celtic v Dundee | 2-0 |
| | Final | Celtic v Rangers | 1-0 |
| 1977-78 | 3rd rd | Celtic v Dundee | 7-0 |
| | 4th rd | Celtic v Kilmarnock | 1-1, 1-0 |
| 1978-79 | 3rd rd | Montrose v Celtic | 2-4 |
| | 4th rd | Celtic v Berwick | 3-0 |
| | Q. Final | Aberdeen v Celtic | 1-1, 1-2 |
| 1979-80 | 3rd rd | Celtic v Raith Rovers | 2-1 |
| | 4th rd | Celtic v St. Mirren | 1-1, 2-3 |
| | Q. Final | Celtic v Morton | 2-0 |
| | Semi | Celtic v Hibs | 5-0 |
| | Final | Celtic v Rangers | 1-0 |
| 1980-81 | 3rd rd | Berwick v Celtic | 0-2 |
| | 4th rd | Celtic v Stirling Albion | 3-0 |
| | Q. Final | Celtic v East Stirling | 2-0 |

|         | Semi     | Celtic v Dundee United      | 0-0, 3-2    |
|---------|----------|-----------------------------|-------------|
| 1981-82 | 3rd rd   | Celtic v Q.O.S.             | 4-0         |
|         | 4th rd   | Aberdeen v Celtic           | 1-0         |
| 1982-83 | 3rd rd   | Clydebank v Celtic          | 0-3         |
|         | 4th rd   | Celtic v Dunfermline        | 3-0         |
|         | Q. Final | Celtic v Hearts             | 4-1         |
|         | Semi     | Celtic v Aberdeen           | 0-1         |
| 1983-84 | 3rd rd   | Berwick v Celtic            | 0-4         |
|         | 4th rd   | East Fife v Celtic          | 0-6         |
|         | 5th rd   | Motherwell v Celtic         | 0-6         |
|         | Semi     | Celtic v St. Mirren         | 2-1         |
|         | Final    | Aberdeen v Celtic           | 2-1         |
| 1984-85 | 3rd rd   | Hamilton v Celtic           | 1-2         |
|         | 4th rd   | Celtic v Inverness Thistle  | 6-0         |
|         | Q. Final | Dundee v Celtic             | 1-1, 2-1    |
|         | Semi     | Motherwell v Celtic         | 1-1, 3-0    |
|         | Final    | Celtic v Dundee United      | 2-1         |
| 1985-86 | 3rd rd   | Celtic v St. Johnstone      | 2-0         |
|         | 4th rd   | Celtic v Queens Park        | 2-1         |
|         | Q. Final | Hibs v Celtic               | 4-3         |

## LEAGUE CUP RECORD

| 1946-47 | Did not qualify in section with Hibs, Hamilton Acas. and Third Lanark. |
|---------|------------------------------------------------------------------------|
| 1947-48 | Did not qualify in section with Rangers, Dundee and Third Lanark. |
| 1948-49 | Did not qualify in section with Rangers, Hibs and Clyde. |
| 1949-50 | Did not qualify in section with Rangers, Aberdeen and St. Mirren. |
| 1950-51 | Won section with Third Lanark, East Fife and Raith Rovers — quarter final — Motherwell (h) 1-4; Motherwell (a) 0-1. |
| 1951-52 | Won section with Morton, Third Lanark and Airdrie<br>Quarter final — Forfar Ath. (h) 4-1; Forfar Ath. (a) 1-1<br>Semi final — Rangers (a) 0-3. |
| 1952-53 | Did not qualify in section with Hibs, St. Mirren and Partick Thistle. |
| 1953-54 | Did not qualify in section with East Fife, Aberdeen and Airdrie. |
| 1954-55 | Did not qualify in section with Hearts, Dundee and Falkirk. |
| 1955-56 | Did not qualify in section with Rangers, Falkirk and Q.O.S. |
| 1956-57 | Won section with Rangers, Aberdeen and East Fife<br>Quarter final — Dunfermline (h) 6-0; Dunfermline (a) 0-3<br>Semi final — Clyde (Hampden) 2-0<br>Final — Partick Thistle 0-0, 3-0. |
| 1957-58 | Won section with Hibs, Airdrie and East Fife<br>Quarter final — Third Lanark (h) 6-1; Third Lanark (a) 3-0<br>Semi final — Clyde (Hampden) 4-2<br>Final — Rangers 7-1. |

1958-59   Won section with Clyde, St. Mirren and Airdrie
Quarter final — Cowdenbeath (h) 2-0; Cowdenbeath (a) 8-1
Semi final — Partick Thistle (Hampden) 1-2.

1959-60   Failed to qualify in section with Raith Rovers, Airdrie and Partick.

1960-61   Failed to qualify in section with Rangers, Third Lanark and Partick.

1961-62   Failed to qualify in section with St. Johnstone, Hibs and Partick Thistle.

1962-63   Failed to qualify in section with Hearts, Dundee United and Dundee.

1963-64   Failed to qualify in section with Rangers, Kilmarnock and Q.O.S.

1964-65   Won in section with Kilmarnock, Partick Thistle and Hearts
Quarter final — East Fife (h) 6-0; East Fife (a) 0-2
Semi final — Morton (Ibrox) 2-0
Final — Rangers 1-2.

1965-66   Won in section with Motherwell, Dundee and Dundee United
Quarter final — Raith Rovers (a) 8-1; Raith Rovers (h) 4-0
Semi final — Hibs (Ibrox) 2-2 Replay 4-0
Final — Rangers 2-1.

1966-67   Won in section with Hearts, Clyde and St. Mirren
Quarter final — Dunfermline (h) 6-3; Dunfermline (a) 3-1
Semi final — Airdrie (Hampden) 2-0
Final — Rangers 1-0.

1967-68   Won in section with Rangers, Dundee United and Aberdeen
Quarter Final — Ayr United (h) 6-2; Ayr United (a) 2-0
Semi final — Morton (Hampden) 7-1
Final — Dundee 5-3.

1968-69   Won in section with Rangers, Partick Thistle and Morton
Quarter final — Hamilton Acas. (h) 10-0; Hamilton Acas. (a) 4-2
Semi final — Clyde (Hampden) 1-0
Final — Hibs 6-2.

1969-70   Won in section with Rangers, Raith Rovers and Airdrie
Quarter final — Aberdeen (a) 0-0; Aberdeen (a) 2-1
Semi final — Ayr United (Hampden) 3-3 — replay 2-1
Final — St. Johnstone 1-0.

1970-71   Won in section with Dundee United, Clyde and Hearts
Quarter final — Dundee (a) 2-2; Dundee (h) 5-1
Semi final — Dumbarton (Hampden) 0-0 Replay 4-3
Final — Rangers 0-1.

1971-72   Won in section with Rangers, Morton and Ayr United
Quarter final — Clydebank (a) 5-0; Clydebank (h) 6-2
Semi final — St. Mirren (Hampden) 3-0
Final — Partick Thistle 1-4.

1972-73   Won section with East Fife, Stirling Albion and Arbroath

Second round — Stranraer (a) 2-1; Stanraer (h) 5-2
Quarter final — Dundee (a) 0-1; Dundee (h) 3-2 (after extra time) Play-off Dundee (Hampden) 4-1
Semi final — Aberdeen (Hampden) 3-2
Final — Hibs 1-2.

1973-74 Qualified in section with Rangers, Arbroath and Falkirk
Second round — Motherwell (a) 2-2; Motherwell (h) 0-1
Quarter final — Aberdeen (h) 3-2; Aberdeen (a) 0-0
Semi final — Rangers (Hampden) 3-1
Final — Dundee 0-1.

1974-75 Won in section with Motherwell, Dundee United and Ayr United
Quarter final — Hamilton Acas. (h) 2-0; Hamilton Acas. (a) 4-2
Semi final — Dundee (Hampden) 1-0
Final — Hibs 6-3.

1975-76 Won in section with Hearts, Aberdeen and Dumbarton
Quarter final — Stenhousemuir (a) 2-0; Stenhousemuir (h) 1-0
Semi-final — Partick Thistle (Hampden) 1-0
Final — Rangers 0-1.

1976-77 Won in section with Dundee United, Dumbarton and Arbroath
Quarter final — Albion Rovers (a) 1-0; Albion Rovers (h) 5-0
Semi final — Hearts (Hampden) 2-1
Final — Aberdeen 1-2.

1977-78 Second round — Motherwell (h) 0-0; Motherwell (a) 4-2
Third round — Stirling Albion (a) 2-1; Stirling Albion (h) 1-1
Quarter Final — St. Mirren (a) 3-1; St. Mirren (h) 2-0
Semi final — Hearts (Hampden) 2-0
Final — Rangers 1-2.

1978-79 First round — Dundee (h) 3-1; Dundee (a) 0-3
Second round — Dundee United (a) 3-2; Dundee United (h) 1-0
Third round — Motherwell (h) 0-1; Motherwell (a) 4-1
Quarter final — Montrose (a) 1-1; Montrose (h) 3-1
Semi final — Rangers (Hampden) 2-3.

1979-80 Second round — Falkirk (a) 2-1; Falkirk (h) 4-1
Third Round — Stirling Albion (a) 2-1; Stirling Albion (h) 2-0
Quarter final — Aberdeen (a) 2-3; Aberdeen (h) 0-1.

1980-81 Second round — Stirling Albion (a) 0-1; Stirling Albion (h) 6-1 (after extra time)
Third round — Hamilton Acas. (h) 4-1; Hamilton Acas. (a) 3-1

Quarter final — Partick Thistle (a) 1·0; Partick Thistle (h) 0·1 (after extra time)

Semi final — Dundee United 1·1; Dundee United (h) 0·3.

1981-82    Failed to qualify in section with St. Mirren, St. Johnstone and Hibs.

1982-83    Won in section with Arbroath, Alloa and Dunfermline

Quarter final — Partick Thistle (h) 4·0; Partick Thistle (a) 3·0

Semi final — Dundee United (h) 2·0; Dundee United (a) 1·2

Final — Rangers 2·1.

1983-84    Won in section with Kilmarnock, Hibs and Airdrie

Quarter final — Aberdeen (a) 0·0; Aberdeen (h) 1·0

Final — Rangers 2·3 (after extra time).

1984-85    Second round — Dunfermline (a) 3·2

Third round — Airdrie (a) 4·0

Quarter final — Dundee United 1·2.

1985-86    Second round — Queen of the South (a) 4·1

Third round — Brechin City (h) 7·0

Quarter final — Hibs (a) 4·4 (Hibs won 4·3 on penalties).

1986-87    Second round — Airdrie (h) 2·0

Third round — Dumbarton (h) 3·0

Fourth round — Aberdeen (a) 1·1 (Celtic won 4·2 on penalties)

Semi final — Motherwell (Hampden) 2·2 (Celtic won 5·4 on penalties)

Final — Rangers 1·2.

1987-88    Second round — Forfar (h) 3·1

Third round — Dumbarton (a) 5·1

Fourth round — Aberdeen (a) 0·1

# EUROPEAN RECORD

## FAIRS CUP

### 1962-63

| | | | | |
|---|---|---|---|---|
| Rd 1 | Valencia | (a) | 2-4 | Mestre (o.g.) Carroll |
| Rd 1 | Valencia | (h) | 2-2 | Verdu (o.g.) Crerand |

## CUP WINNERS CUP

### 1963-64

| | | | | |
|---|---|---|---|---|
| Rd 1 | Basle | (a) | 5-1 | Divers, Hughes 3, Lennox |
| Rd 1 | Basle | (h) | 5-0 | Johnstone, Divers 2, Murdoch, Chalmers |
| Rd 2 | Dinamo Zagreb | (h) | 3-0 | Chalmers 2, Hughes |
| Rd 2 | Dinamo Zagreb | (a) | 1-2 | Murdoch |
| Rd 3 | Slovan Bratislava | (h) | 1-0 | Murdoch |
| Rd 3 | Slovan Bratislava | (a) | 1-0 | Hughes |
| Semi | M.T.K. Budapest | (h) | 3-0 | Johnstone, Chalmers 2 |
| Semi | M.T.K. Budapest | (a) | 0-4 | |

## FAIRS CUP

### 1964-65

| | | | | |
|---|---|---|---|---|
| Rd 1 | Leixoes | (a) | 1-1 | Murdoch |
| Rd 1 | Leixoes | (h) | 3-0 | Chalmers 2, Murdoch |
| Rd 2 | Barcelona | (a) | 1-3 | Hughes |
| Rd 2 | Barcelona | (h) | 0-0 | |

## CUP WINNERS CUP

### 1965-66

| | | | | |
|---|---|---|---|---|
| Rd 1 | Go Ahead Deventer | (a) | 6-0 | Lennox 3, Hughes, Johnstone 2 |
| Rd 1 | Go Ahead Deventer | (h) | 1-0 | McBride |
| Rd 2 | Aarhus | (a) | 1-0 | McBride |
| Rd 2 | Aarhus | (h) | 2-0 | McNeill, Johnstone |
| Rd 3 | Dynamo Kiev | (h) | 3-0 | Gemmell, Murdoch 2 |
| Rd 3 | Dynamo Kiev | (a) | 1-1 | Gemmell |
| Semi | Liverpool | (h) | 1-0 | Lennox |
| Semi | Liverpool | (a) | 0-2 | |

## EUROPEAN CUP

### 1966-67

| Rd 1 | Zürich | (h) | 2·0 | Gemmell, McBride |
|---|---|---|---|---|
| Rd 1 | Zürich | (a) | 3·0 | Gemmell 2, Chalmers |
| Rd 2 | Nantes | (a) | 3·1 | McBride, Lennox, Chalmers |
| Rd 2 | Nantes | (h) | 3·1 | Johnstone, Chalmers, Lennox |
| Rd 3 | Vojvodina | (a) | 0·1 | |
| Rd 3 | Vojvodina | (h) | 2·0 | Chalmers, McNeill |
| Semi | Dukla Prague | (h) | 3·1 | Johnstone, Wallace 2 |
| Semi | Dukla Prague | (a) | 0·0 | |
| Final | Inter Milan (Lisbon) | | 2·1 | Gemmell, Chalmers |

## EUROPEAN CUP

### 1967-68

| Rd 1 | Dynamo Kiev | (h) | 1·2 | Lennox |
|---|---|---|---|---|
| Rd 1 | Dynamo Kiev | (a) | 1·1 | Lennox |

## CUP WINNERS CUP

### 1968-69

| Rd 1 | St. Etienne | (a) | 0·2 | |
|---|---|---|---|---|
| Rd 1 | St. Etienne | (h) | 4·0 | Gemmell, Craig, Chalmers, McBride |
| Rd 2 | Red Star | (h) | 5·1 | Murdoch, Johnstone 2, Lennox, Wallace |
| Rd 2 | Red Star | (a) | 1·1 | Wallace |
| Rd 3 | A.C. Milan | (a) | 0·0 | |
| Rd 3 | A.C. Milan | (h) | 0·1 | |

## EUROPEAN CUP

### 1969-70

| Rd 1 | Basle | (a) | 0·0 | |
|---|---|---|---|---|
| Rd 1 | Basle | (h) | 2·0 | Hood, Gemmell |
| Rd 2 | Benfica | (h) | 3·0 | Gemmell, Wallace, Hood |
| Rd 2 | Benfica | (a) | 0·3 | (Celtic won on toss of coin) |
| Rd 3 | Fiorentina | (h) | 3·0 | Auld, Carpenetti (o.g.), Wallace |

| Rd 3 | Fiorentina | (a) | 0·1 | |
|---|---|---|---|---|
| Semi | Leeds United | (a) | 1·0 | Connolly |
| Semi | Leeds United (Hampden) | | 2·1 | Hughes, Murdoch |
| Final | Feyenoord (Milan) | | 1·2 | Gemmell |

## EUROPEAN CUP

### 1970-71

| Rd 1 | Kokkola | (h) | 9·0 | Hood 3, Wilson 2, Hughes, McNeill, Johnstone, Davidson |
|---|---|---|---|---|
| Rd 1 | Kokkola | (a) | 5·0 | Wallace 2, Callaghan, Davidson, Lennox |
| Rd 2 | Waterford | (a) | 7·0 | Wallace 3, Murdoch 2, Macari 2 |
| Rd 2 | Waterford | (h) | 3·2 | Hughes, Johnstone 2 |
| Rd 3 | Ajax | (a) | 0·3 | |
| Rd 3 | Ajax | (h) | 1·0 | Johnstone |

## EUROPEAN CUP

### 1971-72

| Rd 1 | B.K. Copenhagen | (a) | 1·2 | Macari |
|---|---|---|---|---|
| Rd 1 | B.K. Copenhagen | (h) | 3·0 | Wallace 2, Callaghan |
| Rd 2 | Sliema Wanderers | (h) | 5·0 | Hood 2, Gemmell, Brogan, Macari |
| Rd 2 | Sliema Wanderers | (a) | 2·1 | Hood, Lennox |
| Rd 3 | Ujpest Dosza | (a) | 2·1 | Horvath (o.g.) Macari |
| Rd 3 | Ujpest Dosza | (h) | 1·1 | Macari |
| Semi | Inter Milan | (a) | 0·0 | |
| Semi | Inter Milan | (h) | 0·0 | (Celtic lost on penalties) |

## EUROPEAN CUP

### 1972-73

| Rd 1 | Rosenburg | (h) | 2·1 | Macari, Deans |
|---|---|---|---|---|
| Rd 1 | Rosenburg | (a) | 3·1 | Macari, Hood, Dalglish |
| Rd 2 | Ujpest Dosza | (h) | 2·1 | Dalglish 2 |
| Rd 2 | Ujpest Dosza | (a) | 0·3 | |

## EUROPEAN CUP

### 1973-74

| | | | | |
|---|---|---|---|---|
| Rd 1 | Turku | (a) | 1-6 | Callaghan 2, Hood, Johnstone, Connolly, Deans |
| Rd 1 | Turku | (h) | 3-0 | Deans, Johnstone 2 |
| Rd 2 | Vejle | (h) | 0-0 | |
| Rd 2 | Vejle | (a) | 0-1 | Lennox |
| Rd 3 | Basle | (a) | 2-3 | Wilson, Dalglish |
| Rd 3 | Basle | (h) | 4-2 | Dalglish, Deans, Callaghan, Murray |
| Semi | Atletico Madrid | (h) | 0-0 | |
| Semi | Atletico Madrid | (a) | 0-2 | |

## EUROPEAN CUP

### 1974-75

| | | | | |
|---|---|---|---|---|
| Rd 1 | Olympiakos | (h) | 1-1 | Wilson |
| Rd 1 | Olympiakos | (a) | 2-0 | |

## CUP WINNERS CUP

### 1975-76

| | | | | |
|---|---|---|---|---|
| Rd 1 | Valur | (a) | 2-0 | Wilson, McDonald |
| Rd 1 | Valur | (h) | 7-0 | Edvaldsson, Dalglish, McCluskey, Hood 2, Deans, Callaghan |
| Rd 2 | Boavista | (a) | 0-0 | |
| Rd 2 | Boavista | (h) | 3-1 | Dalglish, Edvaldsson, Deans |
| Rd 3 | Sachsenring Zwickau | (h) | 1-1 | Dalglish |
| Rd 3 | Sachsenring Zwickau | (a) | 0-1 | |

## U.E.F.A. CUP

### 1976-77

| | | | | |
|---|---|---|---|---|
| Rd 1 | Wisla Krakow | (h) | 2-2 | McDonald, Dalglish |
| Rd 1 | Wisla Krakow | (a) | 0-2 | |

## EUROPEAN CUP

### 1977-78

| Rd 1 | Jeunesse d'Esch | (h) | 5-0 | McDonald, Wilson, Craig 2, McLaughlin |
| Rd 1 | Jeunesse d'Esch | (a) | 6-1 | Lennox, Glavin 2, Edvaldsson 2, Craig |
| Rd 2 | Innsbruck | (h) | 2-0 | Craig, Burns |
| Rd 2 | Innsbruck | (a) | 0-3 | |

## EUROPEAN CUP

### 1979-80

| Rd 1 | Partizan Tirana | (a) | 0-1 | |
| Rd 1 | Partizan Tirana | (h) | 4-1 | McDonald, Aitken 2, Davidson |
| Rd 2 | Dundalk | (h) | 3-2 | McDonald, McCluskey, Burns |
| Rd 2 | Dundalk | (a) | 0-0 | |
| Rd 3 | Real Madrid | (h) | 2-0 | McCluskey, Doyle |
| Rd 3 | Real Madrid | (a) | 0-3 | |

## CUP WINNERS CUP

### 1980-81

| Rd 1 | Diosgyeori | (h) | 6-0 | McGarvey 3, McCluskey 2, Sullivan |
| Rd 1 | Diosgyeori | (a) | 1-2 | Nicholas |
| Rd 2 | Politechnica Timisoara | (h) | 2-1 | Nicholas 2 |
| Rd 2 | Politechnica Timisoara | (a) | 1-0 | |

## EUROPEAN CUP

### 1981-82

| Rd 1 | Juventus | (h) | 1-0 | MacLeod |
| Rd 1 | Juventus | (a) | 0-2 | |

## EUROPEAN CUP

### 1982-83

| Rd 1 | Ajax | (h) | 2-2 | Nicholas, McGarvey |
| Rd 1 | Ajax | (a) | 2-1 | Nicholas, McCluskey |

| Rd 2 | Real Sociedad | (a) | 0-2 | |
| Rd 2 | Real Sociedad | (h) | 2-1 | MacLeod |

## U.E.F.A. CUP 1983-84

| Rd 1 | Aarhus | (h) | 1-0 | Aitken |
| Rd 1 | Aarhus | (a) | 4-1 | MacLeod, McGarvey, Aitken, Provan |
| Rd 2 | Sporting Lisbon | (a) | 0-2 | |
| Rd 2 | Sporting Lisbon | (h) | 5-0 | Burns, McAdam, McClair, MacLeod, McGarvey |
| Rd 3 | Nottingham Forest | (a) | 0-0 | |
| Rd 3 | Nottingham Forest | (h) | 1-2 | MacLeod |

## CUP WINNERS CUP

## 1984-85

| Rd 1 | Ghent | (a) | 0-1 | |
| Rd 1 | Ghent | (h) | 3-0 | McGarvey 2, McStay |
| Rd 2 | Rapid Vienna | (a) | 1-3 | McClair |
| Rd 2 | Rapid Vienna | (h) | 3-0 | McClair, MacLeod, Burns |

(Replay ordered by U.E.F.A. after bottle was thrown)

Play-off (Old Trafford)    Celtic 0 Rapid Vienna 1

## CUP WINNERS CUP

## 1985-86

| Rd 1 | Atletico Madrid | (a) | 1-1 | Johnston |
| Rd 1 | Atletico Madrid | (h) | 1-2 | Aitken |

## EUROPEAN CUP

## 1986-87

| Rd 1 | Shamrock Rovers | (a) | 1-0 | MacLeod |
| Rd 1 | Shamrock Rovers | (h) | 2-0 | Johnston |
| Rd 2 | Dynamo Kiev | (h) | 1-1 | Johnston |
| Rd 2 | Dynamo Kiev | (a) | 1-3 | McGhee |

## U.E.F.A. CUP

## 1987-88

| Rd 1 | Borussia Dortmund | (h) | 2-1 | Walker, Whyte |
| Rd 1 | Borussia Dortmund | (a) | 0-2 | |